Oxford School *Shakespeare*

Othello

edited by

Roma Gill, OBE

M.A. *Cantab.*, B. Litt. *Oxon*

OXFORD

UNIVERSI

OXFORD
UNIVERSITY PRESS

Great Clarendon Street, Oxford OX2 6DP

Oxford University Press is a department of the University of Oxford.
It furthers the University's objective of excellence in research,
scholarship, and education by publishing worldwide in

Oxford   New York

Auckland   Cape Town   Dar es Salaam   Hong Kong   Karachi
Kuala Lumpur   Madrid   Melbourne   Mexico City   Nairobi
New Delhi   Shanghai   Taipei   Toronto

With offices in

Argentina   Austria   Brazil   Chile   Czech Republic   France   Greece
Guatemala   Hungary   Italy   Japan   Poland   Portugal   Singapore
South Korea   Switzerland   Thailand   Turkey   Ukraine   Vietnam

Oxford is a registered trade mark of Oxford University Press
in the UK and in certain other countries

British Library Cataloguing in Publication Data

Data available

ISBN 978-0-19-832108-8

10 9 8 7 6 5 4

Printed in Great Britain by Bell and Bain Ltd., Glasgow

The Publisher would like to thank the
following for permission to reproduce
photographs:

P8 Donald Cooper/Photostage; p17 Donald
Cooper/Photostage; p34 Donald
Cooper/Photostage; p43 Donald
Cooper/Photostage; p67 Donald
Cooper/Photostage; p82 Donald
Cooper/Photostage; p97 Donald
Cooper/Photostage; p114 Donald
Cooper/Photostage; p138 Donald
Cooper/Photostage; p158 Shakespeare's
Globe.

Illustrations are by Robert Kettle and David
Cusik (p157)

Cover image by Moviestore.

Oxford School Shakespeare
edited by Roma Gill
with additional material by Judith Kneen

Contents

Introduction

About the Play

The place

The first Act of the play takes place in Venice, which was a powerful city-state in the sixteenth century, important to Europe as a commercial centre and to the whole of Christendom as protector of the Christian faith against Turkish infidels. There are little hints in the first Act of the play which give the impression that Venetian society is orderly, law-abiding and formal: Brabantio appeals to recognized standards of conduct when he angrily confronts Othello in the presence of the duke. Cyprus, the setting for the rest of the play, is far less secure. The island had belonged to Venice for more than a hundred years when, about 1570, the Turks began to attack it. The Turkish invasion of Cyprus led to the famous sea-battle of Lepanto in 1571; and although Shakespeare's play was written more than thirty years after this, his courtly audience in 1604 would have been recently reminded of the battle by a poem on the subject written by their new monarch, James I. Shakespeare uses the Turkish threat (which is not mentioned in his source) as a pretext to move the play's action to Cyprus and to demonstrate Othello's importance to Venice. Once Othello and Desdemona have braved the tempestuous seas, they find enough danger on the island.

A noble character

Othello is a black man in a white society, and a soldier among civilians; he is also one of the greatest lovers in the world's literature.

We learn none of this from the earliest discussion between Iago and Roderigo when they abuse the hated 'Moor', with his 'pride' and his 'thick lips'; later they liken him to 'an old black ram'. So it is a surprise when the Moor appears in company with Iago, whose baseness is immediately revealed when he starts to slander the man who seemed to be his friend. Othello speaks few words at first, and then—with modesty and self-restraint—delivers a speech which, with amazing economy, tells us who and what he is. Othello is a prince, who has done service to the state as the general in command of its military power—it was not unusual for the Venetians to employ foreigners to lead their armies. Othello is confident of his merit, and of his love for 'the gentle Desdemona'. When he is urged to hide from her outraged father, he refuses to run away; he feels secure in the rightness of his position:

> My parts, my title, and my perfect soul
> Shall manifest me rightly.   *1, 2, 31–2*

When he is threatened by the armed Brabantio and his officers, Othello
is calm and relaxed enough to ease the tense situation with a quiet joke

> Keep up your bright swords, for the dew will rust them.   *1, 2, 59*

When Brabantio demands an arrest, and it looks as though fighting wi
break out between the officers and those who support Othello, th
Moor keeps the peace with gentle dignity:

> > Hold your hands,
> Both you of my inclining and the rest.
> Were it my cue to fight, I should have known it
> Without a prompter.   *1, 2, 81–4*

A magnificent character is being created before our eyes. More—much
more—is revealed when Othello defends himself before the duke. He i
respectful to the senators, and begins by telling the truth.

> That I have tane away this old man's daughter,
> It is most true; true I have married her.   *1, 3, 78–9*

Othello's eloquence

As he expands his defence, we become increasingly, and *approvingly*
aware of the difference between Othello and the Venetians. Othello
does not speak like the rest of the characters: 'Rude am I in my speech'
is Othello's description of his own language—but in this he does no
refer to the kind of crude vulgarity which he only learns from Iago as h
falls into his power. Othello does not waste words in polit
circumlocutions (unlike the senators who have been speaking befor
him), and his meaning is never in doubt. His speech has a peculia
grace, which is achieved partly through the rhythms and partly by th
economic use of a precise and powerful vocabulary. It is displayed at it
most eloquent in the description of his 'whole course of love', and th
duke's response to this eloquence must surely speak for all hearers: '
think this tale would win my daughter too.' Othello, we feel, has *lived*
and Desdemona is to be applauded for her choice of husband.

Love is something new to Othello, and his reaction to Desdemon
has a mature intensity that is almost frightening in its richness. As h
tells his story to the duke we can, in the space of some forty lines, watch
the development of this mutual feeling from its earliest days, when a sh

Desdemona hovered near her father's exciting guest, to its full flowering in the declaration:

> She loved me for the dangers I had pass'd,
> And I lov'd her that she did pity them.   *1*, 3, 166–7

The meeting in Cyprus, when Othello is reunited with Desdemona after a perilous voyage, has a sublime happiness which even Othello finds hard to describe: the bliss of heaven cannot equal it. His love has embraced Desdemona, and the two seem to be separate from the rest of the play's characters, in their own world of innocent, joyful loving.

'Honest Iago

But this earthly paradise has its serpent, and we can never forget the presence of Iago. Only we—the audience—can see his machinations. Every one of the other characters is duped by Iago's 'honest' exterior; and, like them, Othello too is deceived by the man whom he knows and trusts. His belief in Iago is quite understandable: after all, he has worked with him for many years, and must have shared the hardships of battle with him. And although Othello has done the state some service, he is still a foreigner in Venice who does not know the customs of the country, whereas Iago is a Venetian, who seems to be wise in the ways of the world and tells his general: 'I know our country disposition well' (3, 3, 203). Othello is 'not easily provoked' into jealousy, but when Iago starts his subtle insinuations it is only too easy for Othello to identify *in himself* the possible reasons that could cause Desdemona's love to waver. Chief of these is his colour: 'Haply, for I am black' (3, 3, 265).

The early scenes of the play emphasize Othello's colour when Iago and Roderigo abuse his 'thick lips', and when Brabantio is revolted at the thought of the 'sooty bosom'. But Desdemona 'saw Othello's visage in his mind', and the duke shares her perception when he tells the angry Brabantio that his 'son-in-law [was] far more fair than black' (*1*, 3, 287). After that, the matter of colour is largely forgotten as Othello is called upon to demonstrate his public authority and his private love. On stage, of course, the reminder is permanently present in the Moor's person. Although it has seemed irrelevant, it matters intensely and is Othello's first thought after he has heard Iago's insinuations.

Suspicion and grief

Othello wrestles with himself, torn between his great love for Desdemona and the doubts, inculcated by Iago, of her faithfulness. Because his love is so great, surpassing all other cares and affections, the thought of its betrayal is equally overwhelming: there is no longer purpose anywhere—'Othello's occupation's gone' (3, 3, 358). His threats to Iago, promising not physical pain but eternal damnation, have a heated violence which is frightening to read—and contrast with the cold, measured lines in which Othello declares his resolution, comparing himself to the sea 'Whose icy current and compulsive course Ne'er feels retiring ebb, but keeps due on' (3, 3, 455–6).

Yet this declaration is not final. Othello must experience more anguish, caused in the first place by Iago's calculated slander. His mental suffering is expressed physically when he falls to the ground in passion: even his body is no longer under control; it is almost as though he becomes possessed by demons. Iago dismisses the frenzy as a commonplace epileptic seizure—'his second fit; he had one yesterday' (4, 1, 51). The excuse may satisfy Cassio—or at least have the desired effect of sending him away from the scene—but it is not an adequate explanation for Othello's distress. There is nothing usual about this episode: Othello's sense of wrong, like his feeling for Desdemona, is of heroic dimensions.

The tragedy

His subsequent conduct towards Desdemona, however, is less than heroic. Having been confronted with Iago's 'ocular proof'—the missing handkerchief—the Moor treats his wife as though she were a loathed prostitute. His powerful love turns to almighty hatred of the supposed deed of adultery rather than the woman herself, for it is the deed which has defeated his highest ideals.

When, at the beginning of the last scene, Othello approaches Desdemona's bed, we see that his love is by no means extinguished. He reacts with acute sensitivity to her warm, sleeping, beauty which he experiences as physically as the scent of a rose—the most potent of all English flowers. His speech (5, 2, 1–22) and the death of Desdemona must surely make the most beautiful of all literary murder scenes! But when his wife lies at peace, Othello must experience the most cruel torture he has so far endured. Emilia, Iago's wife, reveals the truth of the situation, and Othello becomes the most miserable of men. A deeply religious man, he looks at the murdered body and foresees his own punishment—he will be condemned on the Day of Judgement to eternal damnation:

> When we shall meet at compt
> This look of thine will hurl my soul from heaven
> And fiends will snatch at it.   5, 2, 271–3

When the Venetians, Gratiano and Lodovico, begin the process of 'tidying up', Othello is quiet, submissive and repentant. He is arrested, but before he can be removed from the scene he interrupts with a speech that restores his heroic stature and—with a sudden, unexpected, stroke—rescues his nobility. Othello becomes one of Shakespeare's great tragic heroes.

Desdemona's love

In the eyes of Venetian society, Desdemona should have made a highly successful marriage. She belonged to one of the city's noblest families, and could have been the bride of any one of its most eligible bachelors—'the wealthy curled darlings of our nation'. A girl 'so tender, fair, and happy', accustomed to coping with 'the house affairs' for her father, would have made a good wife for any man. She is also sexually attractive (as well as beautiful): all the men who speak of her refer to her ability to arouse them—including Iago, who flirts with her.

But Desdemona has a mind of her own. In the past, before the play opened, she had refused to marry, being 'opposite to marriage' and rejecting the husbands of her father's choice. Now she has met, loved, and married the man of her own heart: she has given herself, body and soul, to Othello—a black man. Her father thought she must be out of her mind, driven to such a mad action by drugs or even witchcraft; but the only magical power used by Othello is his personal magnetism, which drew Desdemona from dreary household chores to learn about a world of adventure and excitement from a man of courage and daring. The colour of his skin did not matter: Desdemona 'saw Othello's visage in his mind', and gave up everything—her father's love, her fortune, and her reputation in the polite society of Venice—to love and live with him.

This is a woman to equal Othello's bravery. As the play unfolds, the different aspects of Desdemona's character are revealed and blend into a unique personality. Her independence asserts itself again when she refuses to stay in her father's house while Othello is away, and begs leave to accompany her soldier husband to the garrison island of Cyprus. She states a magnificently erotic commitment to Othello:

> My heart's subdued
> Even to the very quality of my lord.   *1, 3, 247–8*

When Desdemona arrives in Cyprus, we become conscious of another attribute: we already know of her birth, beauty, intelligence and love—but now Cassio's remarks add a new dimension. He calls her 'divine', and although this may seem the sort of hyperbole that is typical of such a courtier, we can recognize something other in his greeting:

> Hail to thee, lady! And the grace of heaven,
> Before, behind thee, and on every hand,
> Enwheel thee round.   2, 1, 85–7

The quality—grace—which he wishes for Desdemona is difficult t
explain, but it characterizes all her conduct, whether active—in th
things she does—or passive, in her suffering. Shakespeare's concept o
'grace' is a Christian one: theologically it is defined as the supernatur
assistance given by God for the sanctification of the human being.

For a moment the action of the play seems to stand still; then, a
Desdemona accepts Cassio's blessing with thanks, the business begin
again and an anxious wife waits to be reunited with her husband. /
lesser person might have shown her anxiety to those around—bu
Othello's wife must keep her feelings hidden, confiding only in th
audience:

> I am not merry, but I do beguile
> The thing I am by seeming otherwise.   2, 1, 121–2

And once the two are together again, she looks forward to a life of ever
increasing love and happiness.

This, of course, is not to be. Desdemona pleads for Cassio with
fervour that could only come from innocence; she cannot imagine tha
any interpretation, other than her intended meaning, could be pu
upon her words. To suggest that she is being tactless when she persist
in her efforts is to reveal our own sophistication! She bears Othello'
abuse with meekness and patience, allowing only a brief expression o
bewildered bitterness, and never swerving in her love for her husban
The outraged Emilia utters the words that any woman might speak: '
would you had never seen him'; but Desdemona is firm: 'So would no
I'. And her dying words, after declaring her death to be 'guiltless', are a
attempt to divert the blame away from Othello by taking it upon hersel
and speaking a last goodbye: 'Commend me to my kind lord. (
farewell' (5, 2, 126).

Emilia's role

Emilia is in some ways the foil to her mistress, setting off Desdemona'
spiritual beauty by contrast with her earthy commonsense. This i
achieved particularly in the quiet scene (*Act 4*, Scene 3) when she talk
to Desdemona about women and their husbands. If Desdemona i
listening, she does not appear to comprehend Emilia's easy, witty
answers to her troubled questioning. But even the worldly-wise Emili

is blind to her husband's wickedness. She describes, most aptly, the 'eternal villain' who has slandered Desdemona; but she fails to identify him.

Although he abuses her with a rough good humour, Iago's wife has some loyalty and obedience to her 'wayward husband'—enough to pick up Desdemona's handkerchief and give it to him, without knowing why he wants it. But, when she learns the truth of Desdemona's death, even Emilia reaches towards heroic stature.

Iago's motives

Iago is a very different character from all the others in the play. He *seems* to be a friend to all—Othello's trusted 'ancient', Roderigo's ally, counsellor to the downcast Cassio, even adviser to the wretched Desdemona when she has lost her husband's favour. Most praise him as 'honest Iago'; but only to the audience does he show anything of his real self. The rest of the characters have only partial glimpses—and even the audience must make its own judgement on some of the reasons offered by Iago to explain his actions.

He tells Roderigo that he hates the Moor because Othello has chosen another man, Cassio, as his second-in-command, preferring him above Iago. This seems to be the chief motive for his vindictiveness. His anger is that of a man who has been rejected and despised, whose service and experience have been downgraded, and whose career is blocked for lack of paper qualifications. It is, one recognizes, an understandable reaction; but it provokes revenge out of all proportion.

Another motive follows fast upon the exposition of this reasonable disappointment, but this one is wholly irrational: Iago hates Othello because he is black. In the presence of his general, Iago appears loyal and respectful: behind Othello's back, he loses no opportunity to abuse or diminish him. This is the reaction of one who, because he feels himself to be inferior, tries to reduce everyone to his own level.

Frequently in conversation Iago shows this 'reductive' tendency, sneering at Roderigo's passions, abusing women—even the most beautiful and virtuous are good only 'To suckle fools, and chronicle small beer'—and casting doubt on the integrity and competence of his superiors (slandering Cassio for drunkenness, and suggesting that Othello is a regular abuser of his wife).

But nothing describes Iago so well as his own observation when referring to Cassio, he remarks

> He hath a daily beauty in his life
> That makes me ugly.   5,1,19-20

And Iago *is* ugly; in the proverbial saying, he is 'ugly as sin'. The notion that white/black = good/evil is confounded in Iago, who is the ultimate opposite to Othello.

Leading Characters in the Play

Othello   The 'Moor': a black African prince living in a European, colour-prejudiced, society where he holds high rank in the Venetian military forces. As a professional soldier he has had little experience of women.

Cassio   His lieutenant: an honourable Florentine with a weakness for women and drink.

Iago   Othello's ensign (standard-bearer): a Venetian and a professional soldier, he conceals his real nature under an appearance of 'honesty'.

Roderigo   A Venetian gentleman: he is in love with Desdemona, but is being systematically cheated by Iago.

Desdemona   Othello's wife and the daughter of Brabantio; she has married Othello secretly and unknown to her father.

Emilia   Desdemona's lady-in-waiting and Iago's wife: loyal to both her husband and her mistress, she shows an attitude to men that is completely different from Desdemona's.

Brabantio   is Desdemona's father, and a member of the Venetian senate. He is outraged when his daughter secretly marries a black man.

Bianca   Cassio's mistress

Synopsis

ACT 1

SCENE 1 Roderigo and Iago rouse Brabantio from his bed to tell him of Desdemona's rebellion.

SCENE 2 There is a new threat to Venice from Cyprus—but Brabantio demands Othello's arrest for stealing away his daughter.

SCENE 3 Brabantio accuses Othello before the duke, but Othello defends himself. The duke allows the marriage, and commissions Othello with the leadership of the Venetian force against Cyprus. Desdemona asks permission to accompany her husband.

ACT 2

SCENE 1 Storm at sea: the Turkish fleet is scattered, but Cassio arrives safely in Cyprus, followed by Iago and Desdemona. Othello is reunited with his wife, but Iago seems determined to wreck their happiness.

SCENE 2 Othello proclaims a public holiday until evening.

SCENE 3 Iago encourages Cassio to drink until, provoked by Roderigo, he becomes quarrelsome. Othello dismisses him from his office, but Iago advises Cassio to seek Desdemona's assistance. Roderigo threatens to return to Venice.

ACT 3

SCENE 1 Cassio asks Emilia to help him get access to Desdemona.

SCENE 2 Othello sends letters to Venice.

SCENE 3 Iago sows suspicions in Othello's mind until the Moor is convinced that Desdemona is unfaithful to him. Emilia gives Othello's handkerchief to her husband.

Othello: Commentary

ACT 1

SCENE 1   Roderigo and Iago inform Brabantio of Desdemona's secret marriage to Othello. Enraged, Brabantio sets out in search of his daughter.

SCENE 2   Iago warns Othello that Brabantio is searching for him. Cassio brings a summons from the duke demanding Othello's presence at court on a matter of urgent state business. Brabantio accuses Othello of abducting Desdemona, and orders him to be arrested. But the duke's command must be answered first.

SCENE 3   The duke is told about the threatened Turkish invasion of Cyprus, and he welcomes the arrival of Othello and Brabantio. He hears Brabantio's accusation and Othello's defence, sending for Desdemona to testify to her love. The duke tries to pacify Brabantio, and then turns his attention to the Turkish threat. He orders Othello to go to Cyprus. Othello welcomes the command, and Desdemona requests permission to go with her husband. Her request is granted. Roderigo now despairs of ever winning Desdemona's love, but Iago has a scheme that excites fresh hope in him. Roderigo prepares to sail to Cyprus, and Iago speaks his thoughts aloud.

ACT 2

SCENE 1   In Cyprus, Othello's arrival is awaited anxiously, although the Turkish fleet is no longer a threat. Cassio's ship has docked, and then Desdemona arrives, accompanied by Iago. He makes jokes until she is safely reunited with Othello. Iago suggests to Roderigo that Desdemona is in love with Cassio. Left alone on the stage, Iago once again speaks his thoughts aloud.

SCENE 2   The Herald proclaims that there will be free drinks for all, in celebration of the marriage of Othello and Desdemona.

SCENE 3   Iago has got Roderigo drunk, and he now persuades Cassio to drink too much. A quarrel is started in which Cassio strikes Roderigo. Iago sounds the alarm, bringing Othello on to the scene. When Othello hears Iago's account of the fighting, he immediately dismisses Cassio from his office as lieutenant. Othello retires with Desdemona. Cassio grieves over the loss of his position, but Iago comforts him by suggesting that Desdemona will plead with Othello to have him reinstated. Alone on stage, Iago outlines his plan of action, and then assures Roderigo that everything is under control.

ACT 3

SCENE 1   Cassio brings musicians to serenade Desdemona. He asks Emilia (who has been sent out by Iago) to let him see her mistress.

SCENE 2   Othello leaves his quarters to inspect the island's fortifications.

SCENE 3   Desdemona promises Cassio that she will intercede for him. Othello returns with Iago. Desdemona pleads for Cassio, and Othello is not unsympathetic. But when Desdemona has gone, Iago begins his insinuations. He causes Othello to doubt Desdemona and her friendship with Cassio. Desdemona comes to call Othello for dinner, and as she leaves the stage—with her husband—she drops her handkerchief. Emilia picks it up and gives it to Iago. When Othello returns to the scene, he is already very jealous. Iago fans his suspicions, claiming to have seen Desdemona's handkerchief in Cassio's hands. Othello swears that he will be revenged, and orders Iago to kill Cassio.

SCENE 4   Othello asks Desdemona for the handkerchief that she has lost, but she tries to talk to him about Cassio. Othello leaves in a rage. When Cassio comes in, with Iago, Desdemona tells them that her husband is behaving strangely—and Iago goes after Othello. Emilia suggests that Othello may be jealous, but Desdemona declares that he has absolutely no cause for jealousy. As the two women leave, Bianca comes in search of Cassio. He shows her a handkerchief that he has found in his room, and asks Bianca to copy its embroidery.

ACT 4

SCENE 1   Iago persists in his insinuations until Othello, anguished at the thought that Desdemona might be unfaithful to him, falls into an epileptic convulsion. When he recovers consciousness, Iago promises to get proof of what he has been saying. Othello conceals himself, and listens while Iago and Cassio talk about a woman. He assumes that they are discussing Desdemona, and is now convinced of her guilt. Letters recalling Othello to Venice are brought by Lodovico; othello strikes and insults his wife in the presence of this messenger.

SCENE 2   Othello questions Emilia about his wife's conduct. He sends for Desdemona, and accuses her of adultery. She is very distressed. Emilia tries to comfort her, then goes to fetch her own husband. Iago speaks some words of comfort to Desdemona–and then proceeds with his own schemes, setting up Roderigo to attack (and try to kill) Cassio.

SCENE 3   While Desdemona is preparing for bed, she talks to Emilia about unfaithful wives.

ACT 5

SCENE 1   Roderigo (instructed by Iago) lies in wait for Cassio as he comes from Bianca's house. There is a quick skirmish of fighting, in which both Roderigo and Cassio are wounded. The cries arouse othello, who assumes that Iago has murdered Cassio (as he had promised to do in *Act 3*, Scene 3). Lodovico and Gratiano hasten to see what is the matter and Iago also appears on the scene. He takes control of the situation sending Emilia back to Othello and Desdemona.

SCENE 2   Othello comes to Desdemona in her bed-chamber, determined to kill her. He accuses her of having committed adultery with Cassio and although Desdemona pleads her innoccence, he covers her head with a pillow and suffocates her. Emilia brings news of the fighting and the death of Roderigo. When she sees the murdered Desdemona, and hears Othello's accusation, she raises the alarm; this fetches Iago, Gratiano and montano into the room. Emilia denounces Iago, who draws his sword on her and escapes from the scene. He is brought back, however, with Cassio; and the full truth is revealed. Othello, convinced of his own guilt, stabs himself. Iago is arrested and taken away to be tortured.

Time Sequences in *Othello*

On the stage the play moves very fast—a great swirl of activity which is physical, mental, and above all emotional. Quarrels are struck up, hatreds develop, and love flowers and then dies. How long does all this take? In the theatre we are too involved—excited, delighted, frightened, and saddened—to worry about little matters of 'when' and 'how long'. Reading is a slower business, allowing us the time to ask how, for example, could Desdemona and Cassio have the opportunity for adultery, since they sailed from Venice (in separate ships) on the day after the marriage with Othello had been revealed, and seem to have spent only a short time—minutes, perhaps hours—in Cyprus before the arrival of the Moor.

But such questions are irrelevant. When Shakespeare wants us to think about time, as he does in *Act 2*, Scene 3, he gives very clear directions: it 'is not yet ten o'clock' when the scene opens, and early morning when it ends. But when Bianca is berating Cassio for not visiting her, we are meant to be amused at her reproach—not to check her arithmetic:

> What, keep a week away? Seven days and nights?
> Eight score eight hours? And lovers' absent hours
> More tedious than the dial eight score times.   3, 4, 167–9

How can Cassio have stayed away from her for so long? How long has he been on the island? Does it matter?

The dramatist's hours are infinitely more *flexible* 'than the dial'; critics speak very learnedly of 'the double time scheme' in *Othello*, but I suspect there is really only one time scheme—Shakespeare's time—which contracts and expands both the clock and the calendar to suit its own needs.

Shakespeare's Verse

Blank verse

Shakespeare's plays are mainly written in 'blank verse', the form preferred by most dramatists in the sixteenth and early seventeenth centuries. Blank verse has a regular rhythm, but does not rhyme. It is a very flexible medium, which is capable—like the human speaking voice —of a wide range of tones. Easily the best way to understand and appreciate Shakespeare's verse is to read it aloud—and don't worry if you don't understand everything! Try not to be influenced by the dominant rhythm. Instead, decide which are the most important words in each line and use the regular metre to drive them forward to the listeners. Shakespeare used a particular form of blank verse called iambic pentameter.

Iambic pentameter

In iambic pentameter the lines are ten syllables long. Each line is divided into pairs of syllables, or 'feet'. Each 'foot' has one stressed and one unstressed syllable—a pattern that often appears in normal English speech. Here is an example:

> And whát was hé?
> Forsóoth, a gréat aríthmetícián,
> One Míchael Cássió, a Flórentíne,
> A féllow álmost dámn'd in á fair wífe,
> That néver sét a squadron ín the field,
> Nor thé devísion óf a báttle knóws
> More thán a spínster, unléss the bóokish théoric,
> Whereín the tóged cónsuls cán propóse
> As másterly as hé. Mere práttle wíthout práctice
> Is áll his sóldiershíp. But hé, sir, hád the eléction,
> And Í, of whóm his éyes had séen the próof
> At Rhódes, at Cyprus, ánd on óther gróunds
> Christián and héathen, múst be lée'd and cálm'd
> By débitór and créditór; this cóunter-cáster,
> He, ín good tíme, must hís lieuténant bé,
> And Í, God bléss the márk, his Móorship's ánciént.   *1*, 1, 18–33

When Iago begins this description of the man who has been preferred over him, the lines are regular—his hatred is controlled. But soon his anger runs away with him; the normal rhythm breaks sometimes under the stress, and additional syllables crowd into the line. The verse line sometimes contains the grammatical unit of meaning—'That never set a squadron in the field'—thus allowing for a pause at the end of the line, before a new idea is started; at other times, the sense runs on from one line to the next—'knows More than a spinster'. This makes for the natural fluidity of speech, avoiding monotony but still maintaining the iambic rhythm.

Source, Text, and Date

The main source of *Othello* was an Italian story from Giraldi Cinthio's collection *Hecatommithi*, which was popular in the early seventeenth century and available to Shakespeare in both Italian and French (but not English) versions. The play was well researched: Shakespeare borrowed details from a French novelist, Belleforest, and background material from various history books including Richard Knolles' *General History of the Turks* (1603)—which provided the name of a mysterious 'Signior Angelo' whose only mention is at 1, 3, 16, and who is never seen nor heard of again.

The play was probably written between 1603 and 1604; it was performed at court in 1604, and there were later performances at the Globe Theatre, but it was not published until 1622. This first edition was longer than the 1623 Folio edition (Q2), and has more than a thousand differences in wordings, suggesting that Shakespeare must have revised his play for the second edition, adding Desdemona's 'Willow' song and developing the role of Emilia in the closing scenes. This edition (from Norman Sanders's text for the Cambridge Shakespeare, 1984) is based on Q2, since that seems to represent Shakespeare's second thoughts.

Othello

Characters in the Play

The Duke of Venice

Brabantio *a Venetian Senator, father of* Desdemona

Gratiano *a noble Venetian, brother to* Brabantio

Lodovico *a noble Venetian, kinsman to* Brabantio

Roderigo *a Venetian gentleman*

Othello *'the Moor', a general in the service of Venice*

Cassio Othello*'s lieutenant*

Iago *ensign (standard-bearer) to* Othello

Clown *servant of* Othello

Montano *Governor of Cyprus*

Desdemona *daughter of* Brabantio *and wife of* Othello

Emilia *wife of* Iago

Bianca *mistress of* Cassio

Herald

Messenger

Gentlemen of Venice and Cyprus, Sailors, Musicians

Officers, Attendants, Servants

The first Act takes place in Venice; the remainder of the play is set in Cyprus

Roderigo and Iago rouse Brabantio from his
bed to tell him of Desdemona's rebellion.

1 *never tell me*: don't try to make me
believe that; the play opens in the
middle of an argument.
3 *this*: i.e. the elopement of Othello and
Desdemona.
4 *'Sblood*: by Christ's blood; a strong
oath, was omitted in the Folio text.
9 *In . . . suit*: with a personal request.
10 *Off-capp'd*: removed their hats (a sign
of respect).
11 *my price*: what I'm worth.
13 *a bombast circumstance*: some fancy
reason; 'bombast' was a cotton
stuffing used for padding or lining
garments.
14 *epithets of war*: military jargon.
16 *Non-suits*: confounds, rejects the
petition of.
Certes: assuredly.
19 *arithmetician*: theorist; Iago scorns
Cassio because he lacks practical
experience of warfare.
20 *Florentine*: i.e. a foreigner, not a
Venetian. Florence was a centre of
commerce and banking.
21 *almost . . . wife*: 'Who has a fair wife
needs more than two eyes'
(proverbial); in the play it is obvious
that Cassio is not married—perhaps
Shakespeare changed his mind, or
else forgot Iago's early comment.
22 *set . . . field*: position a small
company (about 25 soldiers) on the
battlefield for a formal battle.
23 *devision*: devising, strategic planning.
24 *spinster*: person (usually a woman)
who spins wool.
bookish theoric: textbook theory.
25 *toged*: togèd; wearing official gowns
(like the Roman toga).
propose: give advice.
27 *had the election*: was selected.

SCENE 1

The street outside Brabantio's house: enter Roderigo
and Iago

Roderigo
Tush, never tell me! I take it much unkindly
That thou, Iago, who hast had my purse
As if the strings were thine shouldst know of this.
    Iago
'Sblood, but you will not hear me.
5 If ever I did dream of such a matter,
Abhor me.
    Roderigo
Thou told'st me thou didst hold him in thy hate.
    Iago
Despise me if I do not: three great ones of the city,
In personal suit to make me his lieutenant,
10 Off-capp'd to him; and by the faith of man,
I know my price, I am worth no worse a place.
But he, as loving his own pride and purposes,
Evades them with a bombast circumstance,
Horribly stuff'd with epithets of war,
15 And in conclusion,
Non-suits my mediators. For 'Certes,' says he,
'I have already chosen my officer.'
And what was he?
Forsooth, a great arithmetician,
20 One Michael Cassio, a Florentine,
A fellow almost damn'd in a fair wife,
That never set a squadron in the field,
Nor the devision of a battle knows
More than a spinster, unless the bookish theoric,
25 Wherein the toged consuls can propose
As masterly as he. Mere prattle without practice
Is all his soldiership. But he, sir, had the election,

28 *proof*: proven ability.

30 *be lee'd*: be delayed (like a sailing-
    ship) in calm water ('lee').
31 *debitor and creditor*: a mere book-
    keeper.
    counter-caster: petty accountant (who
    reckons up with tokens or counters).
33 *God . . . mark*: God help us (an
    exclamation of impatience).
    his Moorship's ancient: ensign
    (standard-bearer) to his Moorish
    lordship; Iago shows his obsession
    with Othello's race and colour.

And I, of whom his eyes had seen the proof
At Rhodes, at Cyprus, and on other grounds
30   Christian and heathen, must be lee'd and calm'd
By debitor and creditor; this counter-caster,
He, in good time, must his lieutenant be,
And I, God bless the mark, his Moorship's ancient.

        Roderigo
        By heaven, I rather would have been his hangman.
            Iago
35 Why, there's no remedy. 'Tis the curse of service;
Preferment goes by letter and affection,
Not by the old gradation, where each second
Stood heir to the first. Now sir, be judge yourself
Whether I in any just term am affin'd
40   To love the Moor.
            Roderigo
                        I would not follow him then.
            Iago
O sir, content you.
I follow him to serve my turn upon him.
We cannot all be masters, nor all masters
Cannot be truly follow'd. You shall mark
45   Many a duteous and knee-crooking knave,
That doting on his own obsequious bondage,
Wears out his time much like his master's ass
For nought but provender, and when he's old,
        cashier'd.

35 *service*: military life.
36 *Preferment . . . affection*: promotion
    depends on personal recommendation
    and influence.
37 *old gradation*: old-fashioned steady
    advancement from rank to rank.
39 *term*: way, manner.
    affin'd: bound.

41 *content you*: don't you worry.
42 *serve . . . him*: use him for my own
    advantage.

45 *knee-crooking knave*: bowing and
    scraping servant.
46 *doting on*: enjoying.

48 *provender*: feeding.
    cashier'd: dismissed, sacked.

49 *Whip me*: a contemptuous dismissal.

50 *trimm'd . . . duty*: showing all outward signs of loyalty.

52 *throwing*: bestowing.

53 *lin'd their coats*: made a profit for themselves.

54 *Do . . . homage*: praise themselves.
soul: spirit.

58 *Were . . . Iago*: If I were Othello, I would see what sort of man Iago is.

60 *Heaven . . . judge*: as Heaven is my judge, quite honestly.

61 *peculiar*: personal, private.

63 *native . . . figure*: real act and intention.

64 *complement extern*: outward demonstration.

65 *wear . . . sleeve*: i.e. like the badge of a servant.

66 *daws*: jackdaws (which snap up every trifle).
I am . . . am: I am not what I appear to be.

67 *full fortune*: very good luck.
thick-lips: This insult seems to suggest that 'the Moor' is negroid.
owe: possess.

69 *him*: i.e. Othello.

70 *Proclaim*: denounce.

71 *fertile climate*: prosperous condition.

73 *chances*: opportunities.

74 *colour*: credibility.

76 *like timorous*: such frightening.

77 *by . . . negligence*: caused by negligence at night.

81 *bags*: money-bags.

Whip me such honest knaves. Others there are
50 Who, trimm'd in forms and visages of duty,
Keep yet their hearts attending on themselves,
And throwing but shows of service on their lords,
Do well thrive by them; and when they have lin'd their
        coats,
Do themselves homage: these fellows have some soul,
55 And such a one do I profess myself.
For, sir,
It is as sure as you are Roderigo,
Were I the Moor, I would not be Iago;
In following him, I follow but myself.
60 Heaven is my judge, not I for love and duty,
But seeming so for my peculiar end.
For when my outward action doth demonstrate
The native act and figure of my heart
In complement extern, 'tis not long after
65 But I will wear my heart upon my sleeve
For daws to peck at. I am not what I am.
Roderigo
What a full fortune does the thick-lips owe,
If he can carry it thus!
Iago
                        Call up her father,
Rouse him, make after him, poison his delight,
70 Proclaim him in the street, incense her kinsmen,
And though he in a fertile climate dwell,
Plague him with flies: though that his joy be joy,
Yet throw such chances of vexation on't
As it may lose some colour.
Roderigo
75 Here is her father's house; I'll call aloud.
Iago
Do, with like timorous accent and dire yell,
As when, by night and negligence, the fire
Is spied in populous cities.
Roderigo
What ho, Brabantio! Signior Brabantio, ho!
Iago
80 Awake! What ho, Brabantio! Thieves, thieves!
Look to your house, your daughter, and your bags!
Thieves, thieves!

82s.d. *above*: Some Elizabethan
playhouses seem to have had a
balcony at the back of the stage,
which could be used here to represent
the upper floor of Brabantio's house.

87 *Zounds*: Iago swears by God's wounds.

90 *tupping*: copulating with (Iago uses
the language of sheep-farmers).
91 *snorting*: snoring.
92 *the devil*: In some traditions, the devil
is depicted as black.
grandsire: grandfather.

Brabantio *appears above, at a window*

Brabantio
What is the reason of this terrible summons?
What is the matter there?
    Roderigo
85 Signior, is all your family within?
    Iago
Are your doors lock'd?
    Brabantio
                          Why, wherefore ask you this?
    Iago
Zounds, sir, you're robb'd; for shame, put on your
    gown;
Your heart is burst; you have lost half your soul;
Even now, now, very now, an old black ram
90 Is tupping your white ewe. Arise, arise;
Awake the snorting citizens with the bell,
Or else the devil will make a grandsire of you.
Arise, I say!
    Brabantio
                What, have you lost your wits?

Roderigo
Most reverend signior, do you know my voice?
Brabantio
95 Not I; what are you?
Roderigo
My name is Roderigo.
Brabantio
                                          The worser welcome;
I have charg'd thee not to haunt about my doors;
In honest plainness thou hast heard me say
My daughter is not for thee. And now in madness,
100 Being full of supper and distempering draughts,
Upon malicious bravery dost thou come
To start my quiet.
Roderigo
Sir, sir, sir—
Brabantio
                              But thou must needs be sure
My spirit and my place have in them power
105 To make this bitter to thee.
Roderigo
                                          Patience, good sir.
Brabantio
What tell'st thou me of robbing? This is Venice;
My house is not a grange.
Roderigo
                                          Most grave Brabantio,
In simple and pure soul I come to you.
Iago
Zounds, sir; you are one of those that will not serve God
110 if the devil bid you. Because we come to do you service
and you think we are ruffians, you'll have your daughter
covered with a Barbary horse, you'll have your nephews
neigh to you, you'll have coursers for cousins, and
jennets for germans.
Brabantio
115 What profane wretch art thou?
Iago
I am one, sir, that comes to tell you your daughter and
the Moor are now making the beast with two backs.

---

94 *Most reverend signior*: Roderigo is extremely respectful.
know my voice: the figures cannot be recognized in the dark.

97 *charg'd*: ordered.
haunt: hang.

100 *distempering draughts*: intoxicating drink.
101 *malicious bravery*: mischievous impudence.
102 *start*: disturb.

104 *spirit . . . place*: character and position as a senator.

107 *grange*: isolated country house.

108 *In .. . soul*: with sincere and disinterested motivation.
109–10 *serve . . . you*: i.e. take good advice from someone you dislike.

112 *covered with*: mated with.
Barbary horse: African stallion; the north coast of Africa was famous for horse-breeding.
113 *coursers*: racehorses.
cousins: kinsfolk.
114 *jennets*: little Spanish horses.
germans: blood relations.
115 *profane*: foul-mouthed.

117 *making . . . backs*: having sexual intercourse.

Brabantio
Thou art a villain.
Iago
                              You are a senator.
Brabantio
This thou shalt answer; I know thee, Roderigo.
Roderigo
120 Sir, I will answer anything. But I beseech you
If't be your pleasure and most wise consent
(As partly I find it is) that your fair daughter,
At this odd-even and dull watch o'the night,
Transported with no worse nor better guard,
125 But with a knave of common hire, a gondolier,
To the gross clasps of a lascivious Moor:
If this be known to you, and your allowance,
We then have done you bold and saucy wrongs.
But if you know not this, my manners tell me,
130 We have your wrong rebuke. Do not believe
That from the sense of all civility
I thus would play and trifle with your reverence.
Your daughter, if you have not given her leave,
I say again, hath made a gross revolt,
135 Tying her duty, beauty, wit, and fortunes
In an extravagant and wheeling stranger
Of here and everywhere. Straight satisfy yourself.
If she be in her chamber or your house,
Let loose on me the justice of the state
140 For thus deluding you.
Brabantio
                              Strike on the tinder, ho!
Give me a taper; call up all my people.
This accident is not unlike my dream;

118 *senator*: The actor's tone must determine the sense of his insult.

119 *thou shalt answer*: you will have to pay for; Brabantio speaks (with the insultingly familiar 'thou') to Roderigo.

121 *wise*: informed.

122 *partly*: to some extent (because you seem so unconcerned).

123 *odd-even*: just after midnight.
dull watch: late time.

125 *common hire*: available for general hire.
gondolier: pronounced 'gòndolier'.

127 *allowance*: permission.

128 *saucy*: insolent.

129 *manners*: code of conduct.

130 *have . . . rebuke*: are wrongly rebuked by you.

132 *your reverence*: the respect due to you.

136 *extravagant . . . stranger*: wandering and free-ranging foreigner.

137 *Straight . . . yourself*: immediately find out for yourself.

140 *tinder*: tinder-box.

141 *taper*: candle.

142 *accident*: chance occurrence.

Belief of it oppresses me already.
Light, I say, light!   [*Exit*
  Iago
                              Farewell, for I must leave you.

45 *meet*: fitting; Iago slides away from any risk of discovery.
   wholesome . . . place: good for my job.
46 *produc'd*: called as witness.
48 *gall . . . check*: pull him up sharply (like a horse).
49 *cast*: discharge.
   embark'd: engaged.
50 *loud*: good.
51 *stands in act*: are being fought.
   for their souls: to save their lives.
52 *fathom*: ability.

55 *life*: livelihood.

56 *flag*: appearance. Iago's image is particularly appropriate for an ensign.
57 *That*: in order that.

58 *Sagittary*: Sagittarius; the name of the inn with the sign of the armed Centaur of the zodiac where Othello and Desdemona have taken lodgings.
   raised search: raisèd; search-party he raises.

145 It seems not meet, nor wholesome to my place
    To be produc'd, as if I stay I shall,
    Against the Moor. For I do know the state,
    However this may gall him with some check,
    Cannot with safety cast him; for he's embark'd
150 With such loud reason to the Cyprus wars,
    Which even now stands in act, that, for their souls,
    Another of his fathom they have none
    To lead their business; in which regard,
    Though I do hate him as I do hell's pains,
155 Yet, for necessity of present life,
    I must show out a flag and sign of love,
    Which is indeed but sign. That you shall surely find
        him,
    Lead to the Sagittary the raised search;
    And there will I be with him. So farewell.   [*Exit*

Enter Brabantio *in his nightgown, and* Servants *with torches*

60s.d. *nightgown*: dressing-gown.
61 *despised time*: despisèd; wretched life (scorned by society for his disobedient daughter).
63 *thou*: Brabantio speaks with the affectionate familiar form.

  Brabantio
160 It is too true an evil. Gone she is,
    And what's to come of my despised time
    Is nought but bitterness. Now, Roderigo,
    Where didst thou see her? O unhappy girl!
    With the Moor, say'st thou? Who would be a father?
165 How didst thou know 'twas she? O she deceives me
    Past thought! What said she to you? Get more tapers,
    Raise all my kindred. Are they married, think you?
  Roderigo
    Truly I think they are.
  Brabantio
    O heaven! How got she out? O treason of the blood!

71 *charms*: spells, love-potions.
72 *property*: nature.
   maidhood: girlish immaturity.

170 Fathers, from hence trust not your daughters' minds
    By what you see them act. Is there not charms
    By which the property of youth and maidhood

'Though I do hate him as I do hell's pains' (*1*, 1, 154) David Calder as Iago, Young Vic Theatre, London, 1984.

May be abus'd? Have you not read, Roderigo,
Of some such thing?
Roderigo
                              Yes, sir, I have indeed.
Brabantio
175 Call up my brother. O that you had had her!
Some one way, some another. Do you know
Where we may apprehend her and the Moor?
Roderigo
I think I can discover him, if you please
To get good guard and go along with me.
Brabantio
180 Pray you lead on. At every house I'll call;
I may command at most. Get weapons, ho!
And raise some special officers of night:
On, good Roderigo; I'll deserve your pains.   [*Exeunt*

Scene 2

Othello's lodgings at the Sagittary: enter Othello,
Iago, *and* Attendants *with torches*

Iago
Though in the trade of war I have slain men,
Yet do I hold it very stuff o'the conscience
To do no contriv'd murder. I lack iniquity
Sometimes to do me service. Nine or ten times
5 I had thought to have yerk'd him here, under the ribs.
Othello
'Tis better as it is.
Iago
                              Nay, but he prated,
And spoke such scurvy and provoking terms
Against your honour,
That, with the little godliness I have,
10 I did full hard forbear him. But I pray, sir,
Are you fast married? For be sure of this,
That the magnifico is much belov'd,
And hath in his effect a voice potential
As double as the duke's. He will divorce you,
15 Or put upon you what restraint and grievance

---

176 *Some . . . another*: Brabantio directs the searchers.

178 *discover him*: reveal where he is.

181 *command*: demand help from.
182 *special . . . night*: i.e. not the usual night watchmen.
183 *deserve*: reward.

Act 1 Scene 2
Cassio tells Othello of a new threat to Venice, but Brabantio demands Othello's arrest for stealing away his daughter.

1–5 *Though . . . ribs*: Iago has been giving Othello his own version of the conversation with Roderigo.
1 *trade of war*: as a professional soldier.
2 *very stuff*: essence.
3 *contriv'd*: premeditated.
  iniquity: evil-mindedness.
4 *to . . . service*: for my own good.
5 *yerk'd*: thrust at.

6 *prated*: talked nonsense.
7 *scurvy*: insulting.

10 *full hard*: with difficulty.
11 *fast*: definitely.
12 *magnifico*: Brabantio (the Venetian nobleman).
13 *in his . . . potential*: powerful influence at his command.
14 *double*: influential (perhaps with two votes in the Senate).
15 *grievance*: hardship.

17 *cable*: scope.

18 *signiory*: Venetian ruling powers.
19 *out-tongue*: speak louder.
   to know: unknown.

21 *provulgate*: make known.

22 *siege*: rank.
   demerits: merits, deserts.
23 *unbonneted*: taking off my hat—i.e.
   with all due respect.

26 *unhoused*: unhousèd; unrestrained.
27 *into . . . confine*: under restriction and
   restraint.
28 *yond*: yonder.

29 *raised*: raisèd; alarmed.

31 *parts*: natural qualities.
   title: entitlement, rights (as
   Desdemona's husband).
   perfect soul: clear conscience.
33 *Janus*: Iago swears, appropriately, by
   the two-faced Roman god.

37 *haste-post-haste*: speediest possible.

39 *divine*: guess.
40 *heat*: urgency.
41 *sequent*: one after the other.

The law, with all his might to enforce it on,
Will give him cable.
>   **Othello**
>   Let him do his spite;
My services which I have done the signiory
Shall out-tongue his complaints. 'Tis yet to know—
20 Which, when I know that boasting is an honour,
I shall provulgate—I fetch my life and being
From men of royal siege, and my demerits
May speak unbonneted to as proud a fortune
As this that I have reach'd. For know, Iago,
25 But that I love the gentle Desdemona,
I would not my unhoused free condition
Put into circumscription and confine
For the sea's worth. But look what lights come yond!
>   **Iago**
Those are the raised father and his friends;
30 You were best go in.
>   **Othello**
>   Not I; I must be found.
My parts, my title, and my perfect soul
Shall manifest me rightly. Is it they?
>   **Iago**
By Janus, I think no.

Enter Cassio, *with* Officers *and torches*

>   **Othello**
The servants of the duke and my lieutenant!
35 The goodness of the night upon you, friends.
What is the news?
>   **Cassio**
>   The duke does greet you, general,
And he requires your haste-post-haste appearance
Even on the instant.
>   **Othello**
>   What is the matter, think you?
>   **Cassio**
Something from Cyprus, as I may divine.
40 It is a business of some heat. The galleys
Have sent a dozen sequent messengers

44 *hotly*: urgently.

46 *several*: separate.

49 *makes he here*: is he doing here.

50 *Faith*: in faith, indeed.
boarded: taken possession of.
carrack: treasure ship.
51 *made*: financially secure.
52 *I . . . understand*: we learn later in the
play (*3*, 3, 93–5) that Cassio
accompanied Othello in his courtship
of Desdemona.

53 *Marry*: by the Virgin Mary (a mild
oath).

54 *for you*: ready to fight with you.

This very night at one another's heels;
And many of the consuls, rais'd and met,
Are at the duke's already. You have been hotly call'd for,
45 When, being not at your lodging to be found,
The senate hath sent about three several quests
To search you out.
Othello
      'Tis well I am found by you.
I will but spend a word here in the house,
And go with you.   [*Exit*
Cassio
      Ancient, what makes he here?
Iago
50 Faith, he tonight hath boarded a land carrack;
If it prove lawful prize, he's made for ever.
Cassio
I do not understand.
Iago
      He's married.
Cassio
        To who?

Enter Othello

Iago
Marry, to—Come, captain, will you go?
Othello
        Have with you.
Cassio
Here comes another troop to seek for you.

Enter Brabantio, Roderigo, *and* Officers *with lights
and weapons*

Iago
55 It is Brabantio; general, be advis'd,
He comes to bad intent.
Othello
      Holla, stand there!
Roderigo
Signior, it is the Moor.

Brabantio
                              Down with him, thief!
  Iago
You, Roderigo? Come, sir, I am for you.
  Othello
Keep up your bright swords, for the dew will rust
   them.
60 Good signior, you shall more command with years
Than with your weapons.
  Brabantio
O thou foul thief! Where hast thou stow'd my
   daughter?
Damn'd as thou art, thou hast enchanted her,
For I'll refer me to all things of sense,
65 If she in chains of magic were not bound,
Whether a maid so tender, fair, and happy,
So opposite to marriage that she shunn'd
The wealthy curled darlings of our nation,
Would ever have, t'incur a general mock,
70 Run from her guardage to the sooty bosom
Of such a thing as thou—to fear, not to delight.
Judge me the world, if 'tis not gross in sense
That thou hast practis'd on her with foul charms,
Abus'd her delicate youth with drugs or minerals
75 That weakens motion. I'll have't disputed on;
'Tis probable and palpable to thinking.
I therefore apprehend and do attach thee
For an abuser of the world, a practiser
Of arts inhibited and out of warrant.
80 Lay hold upon him. If he do resist,
Subdue him at his peril.
  Othello
                              Hold your hands,
Both you of my inclining and the rest.
Were it my cue to fight, I should have known it
Without a prompter. Where will you that I go
85 To answer this your charge?
  Brabantio
                              To prison, till fit time
Of law and course of direct session
Call thee to answer.

58 *You . . . for you*: Iago, to protect Roderigo, singles him out from the fighting.
59 *Keep up*: put away.
60 *with years*: because of your age.
62 *stow'd*: hidden.
63 *enchanted*: bewitched.
64 *refer me*: appeal. *all things of sense*: any common sense.
67 *opposite*: opposed.
68 *curled*: curlèd; with curled hair—attractive. *darlings*: favourites.
69 *a general mock*: everybody's scorn.
70 *guardage*: guardianship.
72 *Judge . . . world*: let the world be judge. *gross in sense*: quite obvious.
73 *practis'd*: performed.
74 *minerals*: i.e. poisonous substances.
75 *motion*: will-power. *disputed on*: formally (legally) discussed.
76 *probable*: can be proved. *palpable to thinking*: may very easily be thought.
77 *apprehend*: seize. *attach*: arrest.
78 *abuser*: corrupter. *the world*: i.e. Venetian society.
79 *arts inhibited*: forbidden arts—i.e. black magic. *out of warrant*: unlawful.
81 *at his peril*: at whatever risk to Othello.
82 *of my inclining*: on my side.
84 *will you*: do you wish?
86 *course*: procedure. *direct session*: immediate trial.

Othello
> What if I do obey?
> How may the duke be therewith satisfied,
> Whose messengers are here about my side

90 Upon some present business of the state
> To bring me to him?
> > **Officer**
> > > 'Tis true, most worthy signior;
> The duke's in council, and your noble self
> I am sure is sent for.
> > **Brabantio**
> > > How? The duke in council?
> In this time of the night? Bring him away;

95 Mine's not an idle cause. The duke himself,
> Or any of my brothers of the state,
> Cannot but feel this wrong as 'twere their own;
> For if such actions may have passage free,
> Bondslaves and pagans shall our statesmen be.
> > > > > > [*Exeunt*

90 *present*: urgent, pressing.

95 *idle*: trivial.
96 *brothers . . . state*: fellow senators.

SCENE 3

The Duke's *council chamber: enter* Duke *and*
Senators, *set at a table with lights, and* Attendants

Duke
There is no composition in these news
That gives them credit.
> **First Senator**
> > Indeed they are disproportion'd.
My letters say a hundred and seven galleys.
> **Duke**
And mine, a hundred and forty.
> **Second Senator**
> > And mine, two hundred;

5 But though they jump not on a just accompt—
As in these cases where the aim reports
'Tis oft with difference—yet do they all confirm
A Turkish fleet, and bearing up to Cyprus.

Act 1 Scene 3
Brabantio accuses Othello before the duke,
but Othello defends himself and the duke
gives his blessing to the marriage. Othello
is commissioned with the leadership of the
Venetian force to go to Cyprus, and
Desdemona asks permission to accompany
her husband. Iago reveals his own
intentions.

1 *composition*: consistency.
2 *credit*: credibility.
  disproportion'd: inconsistent.

5 *jump . . . accompt*: do not agree on
  the exact reckoning.
6 *aim*: estimate.

8 *bearing up*: sailing towards.

9 *to judgement*: when carefully
considered.
10 *secure . . . error*: feel safe because of
the inconsistency.
11 *main article*: issue on which they are
agreed.
approve: accept.
12 *In fearful sense*: as a cause for alarm.

Duke
Nay, it is possible enough to judgement:
10 I do not so secure me in the error,
But the main article I do approve
In fearful sense.
    Sailor
[*Within*]   What ho! What ho! What ho!
    Officer
A messenger from the galleys.

Enter a Sailor

Duke
                              Now, what's the busines
    Sailor
The Turkish preparation makes for Rhodes;
15 So was I bid report here to the state
By Signior Angelo.
    Duke
How say you by this change?
    First Senator
                              This cannot be,
By no assay of reason. 'Tis a pageant
To keep us in false gaze. When we consider
20 The importancy of Cyprus to the Turk,
And let ourselves again but understand
That as it more concerns the Turk than Rhodes,
So may he with more facile question bear it,
For that it stands not in such warlike brace,
25 But altogether lacks the abilities
That Rhodes is dress'd in. If we make thought of this,
We must not think the Turk is so unskilful
To leave that latest which concerns him first,
Neglecting an attempt of ease and gain
30 To wake and wage a danger profitless.
    Duke
Nay, in all confidence he's not for Rhodes.
    Officer
Here is more news.

14 *preparation*: force.
makes for: is heading towards.

16 *Signior Angelo*: presumably some
naval commander; see 'Source, Text,
and Date', p.xxii.
17 *by*: about.

18 *assay*: test.
pageant: show, pretence.
19 *in false gaze*: looking the wrong way.

22 *more concerns*: is more important to.

23 *facile question*: easy attack.
bear: overcome.
24 *For that*: because.
brace: readiness.
25 *abilities*: defensive equipment.
26 *dress'd in*: equipped with.
27 *unskilful*: lacking in judgement.

29 *attempt . . . gain*: easy and profitable
undertaking.
30 *wake and wage*: stir up and risk.

31 *in all confidence*: certainly.

Enter a Messenger

Messenger

The Ottomites, reverend and gracious,

Steering with due course toward the isle of Rhodes

35 Have there injointed with an after fleet.

First Senator

Ay, so I thought. How many, as you guess?

Messenger

Of thirty sail, and now they do restem

Their backward course, bearing with frank appearance

Their purposes toward Cyprus. Signior Montano,

40 Your trusty and most valiant servitor,

With his free duty recommends you thus,

And prays you to believe him.

Duke

'Tis certain then for Cyprus.

Marcus Luccicos, is not he in town?

First Senator

45 He's now in Florence.

Duke

                                        Write from us to him

Post-post-haste dispatch.

First Senator

Here comes Brabantio and the valiant Moor.

Enter Brabantio, Othello, Cassio, Iago, Roderigo,
and Officers

Duke

Valiant Othello we must straight employ you

Against the general enemy Ottoman.

50 [*To* Brabantio] I did not see you: welcome, gentle
      signior;

We lack'd your counsel and your help tonight.

Brabantio

So did I yours. Good your grace, pardon me:

Neither my place nor aught I heard of business

Hath rais'd me from my bed, nor doth the general care

55 Take hold on me; for my particular grief

Is of so flood-gate and o'erbearing nature

---

33 *Ottomites*: Turks (from the Ottoman Empire).

35 *injointed*: linked up.
after: following.

37 *sail*: ships.
37–8 *restem . . . course*: steer back to their original course.
38 *frank*: undisguised.
39 *Signior Montano*: the Governor of Cyprus.
40 *servitor*: servant.
41 *free duty*: honourable respect.

44 *Marcus Luccicos*: This person (never mentioned again) may be some knowledgeable Cypriot resident in Venice.

48 *straight*: immediately.
49 *general*: universal (because anti-Christian).

53 *place*: public office.

55 *particular*: personal.
56 *flood-gate and o'erbearing*: torrential (bursting through the 'flood-gate') and overwhelming.

57 *engluts*: engulfs.

61 *of mountebanks*: from quack doctors.

62 *preposterously*: unnaturally.
    to err: to stray from itself.
63 *deficient*: morally defective.
    lame of sense: lacking in intelligence.
64 *Sans*: without.
66 *beguil'd . . . herself*: cheated your
    daughter out of her senses.
68–9 *read . . . sense*: interpret the cruel
    sentence in your own way.
69 *proper*: own.
70 *Stood . .. action*: was named in your
    accusation.
72 *mandate*: order.

74 *part*: defence.

76 *potent*: mighty.
    reverend: respected.
77 *approv'd*: esteemed.

80 *head and front*: height and breadth
    (i.e. the full extent).

That it engluts and swallows other sorrows
And yet is still itself.
    Duke
                Why, what's the matter?
    Brabantio
My daughter! O, my daughter!
    Senators
                       Dead?
    Brabantio
                          Ay, to me.
60 She is abus'd, stol'n from me, and corrupted
By spells and medicines bought of mountebanks;
For nature so preposterously to err,
Being not deficient, blind, or lame of sense,
Sans witchcraft could not.
    Duke
65 Whoe'er he be that in this foul proceeding
Hath thus beguil'd your daughter of herself,
And you of her, the bloody book of law
You shall yourself read in the bitter letter
After your own sense, yea, though our proper son
70 Stood in your action.
    Brabantio
                Humbly I thank your grace.
Here is the man: this Moor, whom now it seems
Your special mandate for the state affairs
Hath hither brought.
    All
                 We are very sorry for't.
    Duke
[*To* Othello] What in your own part can you say to
    this?
    Brabantio
75 Nothing, but this is so.
    Othello
Most potent, grave, and reverend signiors,
My very noble and approv'd good masters,
That I have tane away this old man's daughter,
It is most true; true I have married her;
80 The very head and front of my offending

'Most potent, grave, and reverend signiors' (*1*, 3, 76). Ray Fearon as Othello and Geoffrey Whitehead as the Duke, Royal Shakespeare Company, 2000.

81 *Rude*: plain.
82 *soft phrase of peace*: elegant diction
   of civilians.
83 *pith*: strength.
84 *moons wasted*: months ago.
85 *dearest action*: most important work.
   tented field: camp and battlefield.

87 *broil*: fighting.

90 *round*: plain.
   unvarnish'd: without decoration.

92 *conjuration*: incantations.

93 *charg'd withal*: accused of.

95–6 *her motion . . . herself*: she was
   embarrassed by her own natural
   impulses.
97 *credit*: reputation.

99 *maim'd*: defective.

102 *find out*: suggest.

103 *vouch*: assert.

105 *dram . . . effect*: magic potion
   concocted for this purpose.
106 *wrought*: worked a spell.
   vouch: assert.

107 *more wider*: fuller.
   overt test: obvious evidence.
108 *thin habits*: insubstantial
   appearances.
   poor likelihoods: vague guesswork.
109 *modern seeming*: commonplace
   assumptions.
   prefer: object.
111 *by indirect . . . courses*: by cunning
   and force; forcèd.
113 *request*: consent.
   fair question: honest discussion.

Hath this extent, no more. Rude am I in my speech
And little bless'd with the soft phrase of peace,
For since these arms of mine had seven years' pith
Till now some nine moons wasted, they have us'd
85 Their dearest action in the tented field;
And little of this great world can I speak
More than pertains to feats of broil and battle;
And therefore little shall I grace my cause
In speaking for myself. Yet, by your gracious patience,
90 I will a round unvarnish'd tale deliver
Of my whole course of love: what drugs, what charms,
What conjuration and what mighty magic—
For such proceedings I am charg'd withal—
I won his daughter.

Brabantio
                    A maiden never bold;
95 Of spirit so still and quiet that her motion
Blush'd at herself; and she, in spite of nature,
Of years, of country, credit, everything,
To fall in love with what she fear'd to look on?
It is a judgement maim'd and most imperfect
100 That will confess perfection so could err
Against all rules of nature, and must be driven
To find out practices of cunning hell
Why this should be. I therefore vouch again
That with some mixtures powerful o'er the blood
105 Or with some dram conjur'd to this effect
He wrought upon her.

Duke
                    To vouch this is no proof
Without more wider and more overt test
Than these thin habits and poor likelihoods
Of modern seeming do prefer against him.

First Senator
110 But, Othello, speak:
Did you by indirect and forced courses
Subdue and poison this young maid's affections?
Or came it by request and such fair question
As soul to soul affordeth?

Othello

I do beseech you
115 Send for the lady to the Sagittary
And let her speak of me before her father.
17 *foul*: wicked, culpable.   If you do find me foul in her report,
The trust, the office I do hold of you,
Not only take away, but let your sentence
120 Even fall upon my life.

Duke

Fetch Desdemona hither.

Othello
Ancient, conduct them: you best know the place.
[*Exit* Iago *with two or three* Attendants
And till she come, as truly as to heaven
I do confess the vices of my blood,
So justly to your grave ears I'll present
125 How I did thrive in this fair lady's love,
And she in mine.

Duke

Say it, Othello.

28 *Still*: continually.   **Othello**
34 *moving accidents*: exciting   Her father lov'd me, oft invited me,
   adventures.   Still question'd me the story of my life
   by . . . field: on sea and land.   From year to year—the battles, sieges, fortunes
35 *hair-breadth scapes*: narrow escapes.   130 That I have pass'd.
   i'th'imminent . . . breach: when a   I ran it through, even from my boyish days
   dangerous fortification gave way.   To the very moment that he bade me tell it;
37 *redemption*: ransom.   Wherein I spake of most disastrous chances,
39 *antres*: caves.   Of moving accidents by flood and field,
   idle: barren.   135 Of hair-breadth scapes i'th'imminent deadly breach,
40 *Rough quarries*: rugged precipices.   Of being taken by the insolent foe
41 *hint*: cue, opportunity.   And sold to slavery; of my redemption thence,
42–4 *cannibals . . . shoulders*: These   And with it all my travels' history:
   were often described and pictured in   Wherein of antres vast and deserts idle,
   popular travel books.   140 Rough quarries, rocks, and hills whose heads touch
43 *Anthropophagi*: cannibals, man-eaters.   heaven,
It was my hint to speak—such was the process:
And of the cannibals that each other eat,
The Anthropophagi, and men whose heads
Do grow beneath their shoulders. This to hear
145 Would Desdemona seriously incline;

146 *still*: always.

But still the house affairs would draw her thence,
Which ever as she could with haste dispatch
She'd come again, and with a greedy ear
Devour up my discourse; which I observing

150 *pliant*: suitable, favourable.

150 Took once a pliant hour and found good means
To draw from her a prayer of earnest heart

152 *dilate*: recount in detail.

That I would all my pilgrimage dilate

153 *by parcels*: piecemeal, in parts.

Whereof by parcels she had something heard,

154 *intentively*: listening continually.

But not intentively. I did consent,

155 *beguile . . . tears*: steal tears from her.

155 And often did beguile her of her tears
When I did speak of some distressful stroke
That my youth suffer'd. My story being done,

158 *pains*: sufferings.

She gave me for my pains a world of sighs:

159 *passing*: exceedingly.

She swore, in faith, 'twas strange, 'twas passing strange,
160 'Twas pitiful, 'twas wondrous pitiful;
She wish'd she had not heard it, yet she wish'd

162 *had . . . man*: she had been born a man like that.

That heaven had made her such a man. She thank'd
    me,
And bade me, if I had a friend that lov'd her,
I should but teach him how to tell my story,

165 *hint*: opportunity.

165 And that would woo her. Upon this hint I spake:

166 *pass'd*: endured.

She lov'd me for the dangers I had pass'd,

167 *that*: because.

And I lov'd her that she did pity them.
This only is the witchcraft I have us'd.

169 *witness*: give evidence.

Here comes the lady: let her witness it.

Enter Desdemona, Iago, *and* Attendants

Duke
170 I think this tale would win my daughter too.
Good Brabantio, take up this mangled matter at the
    best:

171 *take . . . best*: make the best of a bad job.

Men do their broken weapons rather use
Than their bare hands.
        Brabantio
                I pray you hear her speak.
If she confess that she was half the wooer,

175 *bad blame*: curse.
176 *Light*: fall.

175 Destruction on my head if my bad blame
Light on the man! Come hither, gentle mistress;
Do you perceive in all this noble company
Where most you owe obedience?

Desdemona

My noble father,
I do perceive here a divided duty:

180 To you I am bound for life and education;
My life and education both do learn me
How to respect you. You are lord of all my duty;
I am hitherto your daughter. But here's my husband;
And so much duty as my mother show'd
185 To you, preferring you before her father,
So much I challenge that I may profess
Due to the Moor my lord.

Brabantio

God bu'y! I have done.
Please it your grace, on to the state affairs.
I had rather to adopt a child than get it.
190 Come hither, Moor:
I here do give thee that with all my heart
Which, but thou hast already, with all my heart
I would keep from thee. For your sake, jewel,
I am glad at soul I have no other child,
195 For thy escape would teach me tyranny
To hang clogs on them. I have done, my lord.

Duke

Let me speak like yourself and lay a sentence
Which as a grise or step may help these lovers
Into your favour.
200 When remedies are past the griefs are ended
By seeing the worst which late on hopes depended.
To mourn a mischief that is past and gone
Is the next way to draw new mischief on.
What cannot be preserv'd when fortune takes,
205 Patience her injury a mockery makes.
The robb'd that smiles steals something from the thief;
He robs himself that spends a bootless grief.

Brabantio

So let the Turk of Cyprus us beguile,
We lose it not so long as we can smile;
210 He bears the sentence well that nothing bears
But the free comfort which from thence he hears;
But he bears both the sentence and the sorrow

---

180 *education*: upbringing.
181 *learn*: instruct me.

183 *hitherto*: so far.

186 *challenge*: claim.

187 *God bu'y*: God be with you.
188 *on*: let us proceed with.
189 *get*: beget.

191 *that*: i.e. Desdemona.
192 *but thou hast already*: except that you have it already.
193 *For your sake*: on your account.
194 *at soul*: in my heart.
195 *escape*: elopement.
196 *clogs*: blocks of wood fastened to the legs of horses to prevent their escape.
197 *like yourself*: on your behalf (and as you would speak if you were not so angry).
lay a sentence: apply a maxim (wise sentence).
198 *grise*: step.
200–1 *When . . . depended*: the troubles are over when there's no hope of cure and we see the worst that until recently we hoped to avoid.
202 *mischief*: misfortune.
203 *next*: best.
204–5 *What . . . makes*: patient endurance makes a mockery of fortune's injuries when these cannot be prevented.
206 *The robb'd*: the man who has been robbed.
207 *bootless*: useless, unavailing.
208 *So*: in that case.
beguile: cheat.
210–11 *He . . . hears*: it's easy to bear this moralizing ('sentence') when a man has nothing else to suffer.

213 *to pay . . . borrow*: has to resort to
    mere patience in order to endure his
    sorrow.
214 *to . . . gall*: whether sweet or bitter.
217 *the bruis'd . . . ear*: the broken heart
    was relieved (by being 'pierced' or
    lanced like a boil) by words.
    pierced: piercèd.
219 *preparation*: armed force.
220 *fortitude*: defensive strength.
221 *substitute*: deputy, i.e Montano.
222 *allowed sufficiency*: recognized
    efficiency.
    opinion: public opinion.
222–3 *a more . . . effects*: which makes
    the final decision in these matters.
223 *throws . . . you*: votes for you as the
    safer choice.
224 *slubber*: tarnish.
225 *more stubborn*: tougher.
226 *boisterous*: violent.
    expedition: assignment.
228 *flinty . . . war*: i.e. sleeping on the
    ground in full armour.
229 *thrice-driven bed of down*: softest
    (winnowed three times) feather bed.
    agnize: acknowledge, confess to.
230 *prompt alacrity*: ready eagerness.
231 *hardness*: hardship.
233 *state*: authority.
234 *disposition*: arrangements.
235 *Due . . . exhibition*: appropriate
    assigning of residence and financial
    support.

That to pay grief must of poor patience borrow.
These sentences, to sugar or to gall,
215 Being strong on both sides, are equivocal.
But words are words; I never yet did hear
That the bruis'd heart was pierced through the ear.
Beseech you now, to the affairs of state.

Duke

The Turk with a most mighty preparation makes for
220 Cyprus. Othello, the fortitude of the place is best known
to you; and though we have there a substitute of most
allowed sufficiency, yet opinion, a more sovereign
mistress of effects, throws a more safer voice on you.
You must therefore be content to slubber the gloss of
225 your new fortunes with this more stubborn and
boisterous expedition.

Othello

The tyrant custom, most grave senators,
Hath made the flinty and steel couch of war
My thrice-driven bed of down. I do agnize
230 A natural and prompt alacrity
I find in hardness, and do undertake
These present wars against the Ottomites.
Most humbly, therefore, bending to your state,
I crave fit disposition of my wife,
235 Due reference of place and exhibition

236 *besort*: companions, attendants.
237 *levels . . . breeding*: is suitable for her social position.

241 *in his eye*: within his sight.
242 *unfolding*: proposal.
    prosperous: favourable.
243 *charter*: public permission.
244 *simpleness*: innocence.

246 *downright violence*: violation of normal standards.
    storm of fortunes: disruption of my own future.
248 *quality*: nature.

250 *valiant parts*: military virtues.

253 *moth*: drone, idler.
254 *rites*: rites of love.
    bereft me: taken away from me.
255 *heavy interim*: sorrowful interval.
    support: endure.
257 *voice*: consent.
259 *palate . . . appetite*: my sexual desires.
260-1 *comply . . . satisfaction*: fulfil with passion the youthful emotions of my own individual satisfaction; Othello believes that he is too mature to be obsessed by sexual passions.
262 *free*: generous.
263 *that you think*: if you should think.
264 *scant*: neglect.
265 *For*: because.
265-6 *light-wing'd . . . Cupid*: love's fleeting trivialities; the god of love is depicted as a winged, blindfolded boy.

With such accommodation and besort
As levels with her breeding.
   Duke
                 If you please,
Be't at her father's.
   Brabantio
           I'll not have it so.
   Othello
Nor I.
   Desdemona
      Nor I; I would not there reside
240 To put my father in impatient thoughts
By being in his eye. Most gracious duke,
To my unfolding lend your prosperous ear
And let me find a charter in your voice
T'assist my simpleness.
   Duke
               What would you, Desdemona?
   Desdemona
245 That I did love the Moor to live with him,
My downright violence and storm of fortunes
May trumpet to the world. My heart's subdued
Even to the very quality of my lord.
I saw Othello's visage in his mind
250 And to his honours and his valiant parts
Did I my soul and fortunes consecrate.
So that, dear lords, if I be left behind
A moth of peace, and he go to the war,
The rites for which I love him are bereft me,
255 And I a heavy interim shall support
By his dear absence. Let me go with him.
   Othello
Let her have your voice.
Vouch with me, heaven, I therefore beg it not
To please the palate of my appetite,
260 Nor to comply with heat the young affects
In my distinct and proper satisfaction,
But to be free and bounteous to her mind.
And heaven defend your good souls that you think
I will your serious and great business scant
265 For she is with me. No, when light-wing'd toys

266 *seel*: stitch up (like the eyes of a young hawk).
  wanton dullness: frivolous blindness.
267 *speculative . . . instruments*: powers of perception in my official role.
268 *disports*: sexual pleasures.
  taint: impair.
269 *skillet*: cooking-pot.
  helm: helmet.
270 *indign*: unworthy.
271 *Make . . . estimation*: attack my reputation.
272 *privately determine*: personally decide.
273 *cries*: calls for.

Of feather'd Cupid seel with wanton dullness
My speculative and officed instruments,
That my disports corrupt and taint my business,
Let housewives make a skillet of my helm,
270 And all indign and base adversities
Make head against my estimation!
      Duke
Be it as you shall privately determine,
Either for her stay or going. Th'affair cries haste,
And speed must answer it. You must hence tonight.
      Desdemona
275 Tonight, my lord?
      Duke
                              This night.
      Othello
                                          With all my heart.
      Duke
At nine i'the morning, here we'll meet again.
Othello, leave some officer behind
And he shall our commission bring to you
With such things else of quality and respect

279 *quality and respect*: importance and relevance.
280 *import*: concern.

280 As doth import you.
      Othello
                        So please your grace, my ancient:
A man he is of honesty and trust.
To his conveyance I assign my wife,
With what else needful your good grace shall think
To be sent after me.
      Duke
                        Let it be so.

281 *honesty and trust*: This is the first time in the play that Iago is verbally associated with the qualities for which he is most highly respected by the other characters.
282 *conveyance*: escort.

285 Good night to everyone. [*To* Brabantio] And noble signior,
If virtue no delighted beauty lack,
Your son-in-law is far more fair than black.
      First Senator
Adieu, brave Moor; use Desdemona well.
      Brabantio
Look to her, Moor, if thou hast eyes to see:
290 She has deceiv'd her father and may thee.
      Othello
My life upon her faith!

286 *virtue . . . lack*: virtue itself is not without delightful beauty; compare 'Handsome is as handsome does' (proverbial).

290 *She . . . thee*: 'He that once deceives is ever suspected' (proverbial).

293 *prithee*: pray you.

294 *in the best advantage*: at the most convenient time.

295 *but*: only.

296 *worldly matters*: business.
direction: instructions.

297 *obey the time*: do what the situation demands.

298–373 The formal dignity of the ducal court gives place to the colloquial cynicism of Iago's conversation with Roderigo.

300 *will*: shall.

302 *incontinently*: immediately.

303 *after*: afterwards.
silly: simple-minded.

306 *prescription*: doctor's order.

310 *Ere*: before.

311 *guinea-hen*: female, prostitute.

314 *fond*: infatuated, foolish.
virtue: power.

315 *A fig*: a contemptuous remark, usually accompanied with an obscene gesture.

318 *set*: plant.

[*Exeunt* Duke, Brabantio, Cassio, Senators,
and Attendants

Honest Iago
My Desdemona must I leave to thee;
I prithee, let thy wife attend on her,
And bring her after in the best advantage.
295 Come, Desdemona, I have but an hour
Of love, of worldly matters and direction
To spend with thee. We must obey the time.
[*Exeunt* Othello *and* Desdemona

Roderigo
Iago.

Iago
What say'st thou, noble heart?

Roderigo
300 What will I do, think'st thou?

Iago
Why, go to bed and sleep.

Roderigo
I will incontinently drown myself.

Iago
If thou dost, I shall never love thee after. Why, thou silly gentleman?

Roderigo
305 It is silliness to live, when to live is torment: and then we have a prescription to die, when death is our physician.

Iago
O villainous! I have looked upon the world for four times seven years, and since I could distinguish betwixt a benefit and an injury, I never found a man that knew
310 how to love himself. Ere I would say I would drown myself for the love of a guinea-hen, I would change my humanity with a baboon.

Roderigo
What should I do? I confess it is my shame to be so fond, but it is not in my virtue to amend it.

Iago
315 Virtue? A fig! 'Tis in ourselves that we are thus or thus. Our bodies are our gardens, to the which our wills are gardeners. So that if we will plant nettles or sow lettuce, set hyssop and weed up thyme, supply it with one

319 *gender*: kind.
   distract: vary.

321 *corrigible*: correcting.

322 *scale*: weighing-pan.

323 *poise*: counterpoise.

325 *preposterous*: unnatural.

326 *motions*: desires.
   carnal stings: fleshly urges.
   unbitted: unbridled.

327-8 *sect or scion*: cutting or graft.

333 *deserving*: deserts.
334 *perdurable*: everlasting.
   stead: help.
335 *Put . . . purse*: prepare yourself
   (financially) for success.
335-6 *Follow . . . wars*: Follow Othello to
   the war in Cyprus.
336 *defeat . . . beard*: Hide your face with
   a false beard (the implication is that
   Roderigo is not man enough to grow
   his own beard).
340-1 *answerable sequestration*:
   corresponding separation.
341 *put but money*: just put money.
344 *locusts*: carobs (a sweet
   Mediterranean fruit).
   acerb: bitter.
345 *the coloquintida*: the bitter-apple
   (colocynth), used as a purgative.
   for youth: for a younger man.
349 *Make*: raise.
   sanctimony: piety.
350 *a frail vow*: Iago is contemptuous of
   the marriage vows.
   erring: a) wandering; b) sinful
   (because non-Christian).
   super-subtle: over-sophisticated.
351-2 *the tribe of hell*: the devils; Iago
   seems to place himself amongst the
   devils.
352 *enjoy her*: i.e. sexually.
353 *clean out of the way*: quite the wrong
   thing to do.
   Seek: prefer.
354 *compassing*: achieving.
356 *fast*: true.

gender of herbs or distract it with many, either to have
320 it sterile with idleness or manured with industry, why
the power and corrigible authority of this lies in our
wills. If the balance of our lives had not one scale of
reason to poise another of sensuality, the blood and
baseness of our natures would conduct us to most
325 preposterous conclusions. But we have reason to cool
our raging motions, our carnal stings, our unbitted
lusts; whereof I take this, that you call love, to be a sect
or scion.

Roderigo

It cannot be.

Iago

330 It is merely a lust of the blood and a permission of the
will. Come, be a man. Drown thyself? Drown cats and
blind puppies. I have professed me thy friend, and I
confess me knit to thy deserving with cables of
perdurable toughness. I could never better stead thee
335 than now. Put money in thy purse. Follow thou these
wars; defeat thy favour with an usurped beard. I say, put
money in thy purse. It cannot be that Desdemona
should long continue her love to the Moor—put money
in thy purse—nor he his to her. It was a violent
340 commencement, and thou shalt see an answerable
sequestration—put but money in thy purse. These
Moors are changeable in their wills—fill thy purse with
money. The food that to him now is as luscious as
locusts shall be to him shortly as acerb as the
345 coloquintida. She must change for youth; when she is
sated with his body she will find the error of her choice.
Therefore put money in thy purse. If thou wilt needs
damn thyself, do it a more delicate way than drowning.
Make all the money thou canst. If sanctimony and a
350 frail vow betwixt an erring barbarian and a super-subtle
Venetian be not too hard for my wits and all the tribe of
hell, thou shalt enjoy her—therefore make money. A
pox of drowning thyself! It is clean out of the way. Seek
thou rather to be hanged in compassing thy joy than to
355 be drowned and go without her.

Roderigo

Wilt thou be fast to my hopes if I depend on the issue?

359 *hearted*: sincere, heart-felt.
359–60 *be conjunctive*: join together.

363 *delivered*: brought to birth.
Traverse!: about turn (a military term).

367 *betimes*: early.

374–95 Iago's soliloquy now uses the intimacy of verse.
374 *ever*: always.
my fool my purse: make a profit out of a fool.
375 *gain'd knowledge*: experience.
profane: abuse.
376 *expend*: waste.
snipe: worthless bird (a long-billed marsh bird).
377 *But*: only.
378 *abroad*: generally.
'twixt my sheets: in my bed.
379 *He's . . . office*: i.e. he has slept with my wife.
380 *kind*: regard.
381 *surety*: certainty.
holds me well: esteems me.
382 *purpose*: plan.
384 *place*: position.
plume . . . will: put a feather in my cap.

Iago
Thou art sure of me. Go make money. I have told thee
often, and I retell thee again and again, I hate the Moor.
My cause is hearted: thine hath no less reason. Let us be
360 conjunctive in our revenge against him. If thou canst
cuckold him, thou dost thyself a pleasure, me a sport.
There are many events in the womb of time which will
be delivered. Traverse! Go, provide thy money. We will
have more of this tomorrow. Adieu.

Roderigo
365 Where shall we meet i'the morning?

Iago
At my lodging.

Roderigo
I'll be with thee betimes.

Iago
Go to; farewell. Do you hear, Roderigo?

Roderigo
What say you?

Iago
370 No more of drowning, do you hear?

Roderigo
I am changed.

Iago
Go to; farewell. Put money enough in your purse.

Roderigo
I'll sell all my land.   [*Exit*

Iago
Thus do I ever make my fool my purse;
375 For I mine own gain'd knowledge should profane
If I would time expend with such a snipe
But for my sport and profit. I hate the Moor,
And it is thought abroad that 'twixt my sheets
He's done my office. I know not if't be true
380 Yet I, for mere suspicion in that kind,
Will do as if for surety. He holds me well:
The better shall my purpose work on him.
Cassio's a proper man: let me see now;
To get his place and to plume up my will
385 In double knavery. How? How? Let's see.

386 *abuse*: deceive.

387 *he*: i.e. Cassio.

388 *person*: agreeable appearance.
     smooth dispose: charming manner.

389 *To be suspected*: to arouse suspicion.
     fram'd: designed.

390 *free and open*: honest and trusting.

392–3 *as . . . are*: proverbial.

394 *engender'd*: conceived.

After some time, to abuse Othello's ear
That he is too familiar with his wife;
He hath a person and a smooth dispose
To be suspected, fram'd to make women false.
390 The Moor is of a free and open nature,
That thinks men honest that but seem to be so,
And will as tenderly be led by the nose
As asses are.
I have't. It is engender'd. Hell and night
395 Must bring this monstrous birth to the world's light.
                                          [*Exit*

Act 2 Scene 1

Storm at sea. News is brought to Montano
and two gentlemen that the Turkish fleet is
scattered. Cassio arrives safely in Cyprus,
followed by Desdemona and Iago who wait
anxiously for Othello. Soon husband and
wife are reunited—but Iago seems
determined to wreck their happiness.

2 *high-wrought flood*: tempestuous sea.

4 *Descry*: perceive, detect.

7 *ruffian'd*: raged.
8 *ribs of oak*: wooden ship's sides.
  mountains: mountainous seas.
9 *hold the mortise*: keep their joints
  intact.

SCENE 1

Cyprus: enter Montano *and two* Gentlemen

Montano
What from the cape can you discern at sea?
  First Gentleman
Nothing at all; it is a high-wrought flood.
I cannot 'twixt the heaven and the main
Descry a sail.
  Montano
5 Methinks the wind does speak aloud at land,
A fuller blast ne'er shook our battlements.
If it hath ruffian'd so upon the sea,
What ribs of oak, when mountains melt on them,
Can hold the mortise? What shall we hear of this?

10 *segregation*: scattering.

11 *banning*: forbidding (refusing entry to
the waves).
shore: coast-line.

12 *The . . . clouds*: the wave, rebuked by
the shore, seems to throw itself at the
sky.

13 *monstrous mane*: mane like some wild
monster (punning on 'main' = sea).

14 *Bear*: the constellation Ursa Minor.

15 *guards*: the two bright stars in this
constellation were known as the
'Guardians'.
fixed: fixèd.
Pole: pole star.

16 *like molestation*: similar upheaval.

17 *enchafed flood*: enchafèd; enraged
sea.

18 *enshelter'd and embay'd*: sheltered in
some bay.

19 *bear it out*: weather the storm.

22 *their . . . halts*: their enterprise is
crippled.

23 *sufferance*: damage.

26 *Veronesa*: Perhaps this was a ship
fitted out in Verona, or some light
single-masted cutter (so-called from
the Italian *verrinare* = to cut through).

32 *Touching*: about.
sadly: anxiously.

36 *full*: perfect.

Second Gentleman

10 A segregation of the Turkish fleet:
For do but stand upon the banning shore,
The chidden billow seems to pelt the clouds;
The wind-shak'd surge, with high and monstrous
      mane,
Seems to cast water on the burning Bear

15 And quench the guards of th'ever-fixed Pole.
I never did like molestation view
On the enchafed flood.

Montano
                                  If that the Turkish fleet
Be not enshelter'd and embay'd, they are drown'd:
It is impossible they bear it out.

Enter a third Gentleman

Third Gentleman

20 News, lads! Our wars are done:
The desperate tempest hath so bang'd the Turks
That their designment halts. A noble ship of Venice
Hath seen a grievous wrack and sufferance
On most part of their fleet.

Montano

25 How? Is this true?

Third Gentleman
                        The ship is here put in,
A Veronesa; Michael Cassio,
Lieutenant to the warlike Moor Othello,
Is come on shore; the Moor himself at sea,
And is in full commission here for Cyprus.

Montano

30 I am glad on't; 'tis a worthy governor.

Third Gentleman
But this same Cassio, though he speak of comfort
Touching the Turkish loss, yet he looks sadly
And prays the Moor be safe; for they were parted
With foul and violent tempest.

Montano
                                  Pray heaven he be;

35 For I have serv'd him, and the man commands
Like a full soldier. Let's to the seaside, ho!

As well to see the vessel that's come in
As to throw out our eyes for brave Othello,

39–40 *the main . . . regard*: the sea and
the blue of the sky indistinguishable.

Even till we make the main and th'aerial blue
40 An indistinct regard.
>   **Third Gentleman**
>   Come, let's do so;
>   For every minute is expectancy

42 *arrivance*: arrivals.

Of more arrivance.

Enter Cassio

Cassio
Thanks, you the valiant of this warlike isle

44 *approve*: speak well of.

That so approve the Moor. O, let the heavens
45 Give him defence against the elements,
For I have lost him on a dangerous sea.
>   **Montano**

47 *Is . . . shipp'd?*: does he have a good
ship?

Is he well shipp'd?
>   **Cassio**

48 *bark*: vessel.
49 *approv'd allowance*: tested experience.

His bark is stoutly timber'd, and his pilot
Of very expert and approv'd allowance;

50–1 *not . . . cure*: without being
excessively optimistic, are
nevertheless confident.

50 Therefore my hopes, not surfeited to death,
Stand in bold cure.

51s.d. *within*: offstage.

A shout within, 'A sail, a sail, a sail!'

Enter a Messenger

Cassio
What noise?
>   **Messenger**

53 *brow o'the sea*: cliff edge.

The town is empty; on the brow o'the sea
Stand ranks of people and they cry, 'A sail!'
>   **Cassio**

55 *My . . . for*: I hope it is.

55 My hopes do shape him for the governor.

A shot is heard within

Second Gentleman

56 *discharge . . . courtesy*: fire a friendly
shot.

They do discharge their shot of courtesy;
Our friends at least.

77143

Cassio

                    I pray you, sir, go forth,
And give us truth who 'tis that is arriv'd.

Second Gentleman

I shall.   [*Exit*

Montano

60 But, good lieutenant, is your general wiv'd?

Cassio

Most fortunately: he hath achiev'd a maid
That paragons description and wild fame;
One that excels the quirks of blazoning pens
And in th'essential vesture of creation

65 Does tire the ingener.

Enter Second Gentleman

                    How now? Who's put in?

Second Gentleman

'Tis one Iago, ancient to the general.

Cassio

He's had most favourable and happy speed:
Tempests themselves, high seas, and howling winds,
The gutter'd rocks and congregated sands,

70 Traitors enscarp'd to clog the guiltless keel,
As having sense of beauty do omit
Their mortal natures, letting go safely by
The divine Desdemona.

Montano

                        What is she?

Cassio

She that I spake of, our great captain's captain,

75 Left in the conduct of the bold Iago,
Whose footing here anticipates our thoughts
A se'nnight's speed. Great Jove Othello guard
And swell his sail with thine own powerful breath,
That he may bless this bay with his tall ship,

80 Make love's quick pants in Desdemona's arms,
Give renew'd fire to our extincted spirits,
And bring all Cyprus comfort.

---

58 *give us truth*: find out for certain.

60 *wiv'd*: married.

62 *paragons*: beats.
    fame: rumour.
63 *quirks*: fantasies.
    blazoning: describing; the word is
    particularly used in heraldry.
64 *essential . . . creation*: in the perfect
    beauty of her created being.
65 *tire the ingener*: exhaust the creative
    artist, transcend the imagination.

69 *gutter'd*: jagged.
    congregated sands: sandbanks.
70 *enscarp'd*: ridged along.
    guiltless keel: unwary ship.
71 *As having sense*: as though conscious.
71–2 *omit . . . natures*: refrain from using
    their natural powers.

76 *footing*: landing.
76–7 *anticipates . . . speed*: is a week
    earlier than we expected.

79 *tall ship*: galleon.

81 *extincted*: extinguished, depressed.

Enter Desdemona, Iago, Emilia, *and* Roderigo

87 *Enwheel*: encircle.

> O, behold,
> The riches of the ship is come on shore!
> You men of Cyprus, let her have your knees.
> 85 Hail to thee, lady! And the grace of heaven,
> Before, behind thee, and on every hand,
> Enwheel thee round.

Desdemona

88 *tidings*: news.

> I thank you, valiant Cassio.
> What tidings can you tell me of my lord?

Cassio

89 *aught*: anything.

> He is not yet arriv'd; nor know I aught
> 90 But that he's well, and will be shortly here.

Desdemona

> O, but I fear—how lost you company?

Cassio

92 *contention*: battle.

> The great contention of the sea and skies
> Parted our fellowship.

A shout within, 'A sail, a sail!' A shot is heard

> But hark, a sail!

Second Gentleman

94 *give their greeting*: salute (by firing a salvo).

> They give their greeting to the citadel:
> 95 This likewise is a friend.

Cassio

> See for the news.
> [*Exit* Second Gentleman
> Good ancient, you are welcome [*To* Emilia] Welcome,
>   mistress.

97 *gall*: annoy.
98 *extend*: give an elaborate greeting.
  breeding: the way I was brought up.
99 *bold*: confident.

> Let it not gall your patience, good Iago,
> That I extend my manners. 'Tis my breeding
> That gives me this bold show of courtesy.

He kisses Emilia

Iago

> 100 Sir, would she give you so much of her lips
> As of her tongue she oft bestows on me
> You would have enough.

'Good ancient, you are welcome. Welcome, mistress' (2, 1, 96). Zoe Waites as Desdemona, Richard McCabe as Iago, Henry Ian Cusick as Cassio, and Rachel Joyce as Emilia, Royal Shakespeare Company, 2000.

Desdemona
Alas, she has no speech.
    Iago
                              In faith, too much:
I find it still when I have list to sleep.
105 Marry, before your ladyship, I grant
She puts her tongue a little in her heart
And chides with thinking.
    Emilia
                              You've little cause to say so.
    Iago
Come on, come on; you are pictures out of doors, bells
in your parlours, wild-cats in your kitchens, saints in
110 your injuries, devils being offended, players in your
housewifery, and housewives in your beds.
    Desdemona
O fie upon thee, slanderer!
    Iago
Nay, it is true, or else I am a Turk:
You rise to play and go to bed to work.
    Emilia
115 You shall not write my praise.
    Iago
                              No, let me not.
    Desdemona
What wouldst thou write of me, if thou shouldst praise
    me?
    Iago
O, gentle lady, do not put me to't,
For I am nothing if not critical.
    Desdemona
Come on, assay. There's one gone to the harbour?
    Iago
120 Ay, madam.
    Desdemona
[*Aside*] I am not merry, but I do beguile
The thing I am by seeming otherwise—
Come, how wouldst thou praise me?
    Iago
I am about it, but indeed my invention
125 Comes from my pate as birdlime does from frieze—

04 *still*: always.
    list: a desire.
05 *before*: in the presence of.
06–7 *puts . . . thinking*: keeps her tongue
    to herself and only thinks spiteful
    thoughts.

08 *pictures*: silent images.
    bells: i.e. noisy.
10 *injuries*: sufferings (real or imaginary).
    players: deceivers.
11 *housewives*: (pronounced 'hussifs')
    prostitutes.

13 *Turk*: infidel (whose word was not to
    be believed).

19 *assay*: make an attempt.
    one: somebody.

21 *beguile*: disguise.

25 *pate*: head.
    birdlime: a sticky substance used to
    trap birds.
    frieze: a coarse woollen fabric.

126 *labours*: a) works hard; b) is giving birth.

130 *black*: with dark hair and skin.
witty: quick to understand.

132 *white*: a) fair lover; b) man ('wight').
fit: match, equal.

135 *folly*: a) foolishness; b) wantonness.

138 *foul*: plain, ugly.

139 *thereunto*: in addition.

144 *put on the vouch*: compel the approval.

145 *ever*: always.

146 *Had . . . will*: spoke easily.

147 *gay*: garish.

148 *Fled . . . may"*: did not do as she wished, yet knew when she might do so.

149 *nigh*: possible.

150 *Bade . . . stay*: accepted her injury.

152 *change . . . tail*: accept a worthless object for something valuable (with sexual innuendo: 'cod's head' and 'tail' = male and female genitals).

155 *wight*: person.

It plucks out brains and all. But my muse labours,
And thus she is deliver'd:
'If she be fair and wise, fairness and wit,
The one's for use, the other useth it.'

Desdemona
130 Well prais'd! How if she be black and witty?

Iago
'If she be black, and thereto have a wit,
She'll find a white that shall her blackness fit.'

Desdemona
Worse and worse.

Emilia
                                    How if fair and foolish?

Iago
'She never yet was foolish that was fair,
135 For even her folly help'd her to an heir.'

Desdemona
These are old fond paradoxes to make fools laugh
i'th'alehouse. What miserable praise hast thou for her
that's foul and foolish?

Iago
'There's none so foul and foolish thereunto,
140 But does foul pranks which fair and wise ones do.'

Desdemona
O heavy ignorance! Thou praisest the worst best. But
what praise couldst thou bestow on a deserving woman
indeed? One that in the authority of her merit did justly
put on the vouch of very malice itself?

Iago
145 'She that was ever fair, and never proud,
Had tongue at will, and yet was never loud;
Never lack'd gold, and yet went never gay;
Fled from her wish, and yet said "Now I may";
She that being anger'd, her revenge being nigh,
150 Bade her wrong stay, and her displeasure fly;
She that in wisdom never was so frail
To change the cod's head for the salmon's tail;
She that could think and ne'er disclose her mind,
See suitors following and not look behind;
155 She was a wight, if ever such wight were—'

157 *chronicle . . . beer*: keep household
    accounts.

160 *profane and liberal*: coarse and
    licentious.

161 *home*: plainly, directly.
    relish . . . in: appreciate him better
    as.

163 *well said*: well done.

165 *gyve*: fetter.
166 *courtship*: courtly behaviour.
169 *apt . . . in*: prone to behave like a fine
    gentleman.
171 *Would*: I wish.
172 *clyster-pipes*: enema syringes.
173 *his trumpet*: his personal trumpet-call.

Desdemona
To do what?
    Iago
'To suckle fools and chronicle small beer.'
    Desdemona
O, most lame and impotent conclusion! Do not learn of
him, Emilia, though he be thy husband. How say you,

160 Cassio, is he not a most profane and liberal counsellor?
    Cassio
He speaks home, madam; you may relish him more in
the soldier than in the scholar.
    Iago
[*Aside*] He takes her by the palm. Ay, well said; whisper.
With as little a web as this will I ensnare as great a fly as

165 Cassio. Ay, smile upon her, do. I will gyve thee in thine
own courtship. You say true, 'tis so indeed. If such tricks
as these strip you out of your lieutenantry, it had been
better you had not kissed your three fingers so oft,
which now again you are most apt to play the sir in. Very

170 good, well kissed, an excellent courtesy! 'Tis so indeed.
Yet again your fingers to your lips? Would they were
clyster-pipes for your sake!

Trumpets within

The Moor! I know his trumpet.
    Cassio
                              'Tis truly so.
    Desdemona
Let's meet him and receive him.
    Cassio
                            Lo, where he comes!

Enter Othello *and* Attendants

    Othello
175 O, my fair warrior!
    Desdemona
                    My dear Othello!

Othello

It gives me wonder great as my content
To see you here before me. O, my soul's joy,
If after every tempest come such calms,
May the winds blow till they have waken'd death,
180 And let the labouring bark climb hills of seas,
Olympus-high, and duck again as low
As hell's from heaven. If it were now to die,
'Twere now to be most happy; for I fear
My soul hath her content so absolute
185 That not another comfort like to this
Succeeds in unknown fate.

Desdemona
                                    The heavens forbid
But that our loves and comforts should increase,
Even as our days do grow.

Othello
                                    Amen to that, sweet powers!
I cannot speak enough of this content;
190 It stops me here; it is too much of joy.

They kiss

And this, and this, the greatest discords be
That e'er our hearts shall make.

Iago
[*Aside*]   O, you are well tun'd now!
But I'll set down the pegs that make this music,
As honest as I am.

Othello
                                    Come, let us to the castle.
195 News, friends; our wars are done; the Turks are
        drown'd.
How does my old acquaintance of this isle?
Honey, you shall be well desir'd in Cyprus;
I have found great love amongst them. O my sweet,
I prattle out of fashion and I dote
200 In mine own comforts. I prithee, good Iago,
Go to the bay and disembark my coffers;
Bring thou the master to the citadel;
He is a good one, and his worthiness

---

180 *labouring bark*: struggling ship.
181 *Olympus-high*: As high as Mount Olympus, home of the classical gods. *duck*: dive down.
182 *it were now to die*: I were to die now.
184 *content*: happiness. *absolute*: perfect.
186 *Succeeds*: follows. *unknown fate*: the life to come.

188 *as . . . grow*: as long as our lives last. *Amen*: Othello responds to Desdemona's prayer.

190 *stops me here*: chokes me.

191 *this*: i.e. the kiss. *be*: may be.

192–3 *well . . . music*: Iago continues Othello's musical imagery.
193 *set down the pegs*: loosen the screws (of a musical instrument like the lute).

197 *Honey*: A term of affection for Desdemona. *well desir'd*: well received.
199 *I prattle . . . fashion*: I shouldn't be talking like this.
199–200 *I dote . . . comforts*: lose myself in my own happiness.
201 *disembark my coffers*: unload my luggage.
202 *master*: i.e. of the ship.

204 *challenge*: demand.

206 *presently*: shortly.

209 *is . . . them*: they are born with.
210 *list*: listen.
210–11 *watches . . . guard*: is on night-
　　duty in the guard-house.
211 *directly*: certainly.

214 *thus*: i.e. on your lips.

215 *but*: only.

217 *still*: continually.

219 *blood*: passion.
220 *act of sport*: sexual intercourse.
221 *favour*: appearance.
222 *sympathy*: agreement.
223–4 *required conveniences*: essential
　　conditions.
224 *tenderness*: sensitivity.
225 *abused*: disgusted.
　　heave the gorge: vomit.
226 *Very nature*: natural reactions
　　themselves.
228 *pregnant . . . position*: obvious and
　　natural assumption.
229 *in the degree*: next in line.
230 *voluble*: smooth-tongued.
　　conscionable: conscientious.
231 *humane*: polite.
232 *compassing*: achieving.
　　salt: lecherous.
233 *slipper*: slippery.
234 *occasions*: opportunities.
235 *stamp*: coin, forge.

238 *green*: unripe, immature.
239 *found*: recognized his intentions.

Does challenge much respect. Come, Desdemona,
205 Once more well met at Cyprus!

　　　　　[*Exeunt all except* Iago *and* Roderigo

Iago

[*To a departing* Attendant] Do thou meet me presently
at the harbour. [*To* Roderigo] Come hither. If thou be'st
valiant—as they say base men being in love have then a
nobility in their natures more than is native to them—
210 list me. The lieutenant tonight watches on the court of
guard. First, I must tell thee this: Desdemona is directly
in love with him.

Roderigo

With him? Why, 'tis not possible!

Iago

Lay thy finger thus, and let thy soul be instructed. Mark
215 me with what violence she first loved the Moor but for
bragging and telling her fantastical lies. And will she
love him still for prating? Let not thy discreet heart
think it. Her eye must be fed. And what delight shall she
have to look on the devil? When the blood is made dull
220 with the act of sport, there should be, again to inflame it
and to give satiety a fresh appetite, loveliness in favour,
sympathy in years, manners, and beauties: all which the
Moor is defective in. Now for want of these required
conveniences, her delicate tenderness will find itself
225 abused, begin to heave the gorge, disrelish and abhor
the Moor. Very nature will instruct her in it, and compel
her to some second choice. Now, sir, this granted—as it
is a most pregnant and unforced position—who stands
so eminent in the degree of this fortune as Cassio
230 does?—a knave very voluble; no further conscionable
than in putting on the mere form of civil and humane
seeming for the better compassing of his salt and most
hidden loose affection. Why none; why none—a slipper
and subtle knave, a finder out of occasions, that has an
235 eye can stamp and counterfeit advantages, though true
advantage never present itself; a devilish knave! Besides,
the knave is handsome, young, and hath all those
requisites in him that folly and green minds look after.
A pestilent complete knave; and the woman hath found
240 him already.

241–2 *blest condition*: heavenly innocence.

243 *fig's end*: rubbish; the exclamation would be accompanied by an obscene gesture.
The wine . . . grapes: i.e. she's only human.
245 *pudding*: nonsense.
245–6 *paddle with*: caress.

248 *index*: indicator.
obscure: cryptic.

251 *mutualities*: reciprocal intimacies.
252 *marshal*: lead.
hard at hand: close behind.
253 *incorporate*: bodily.
254 *be . . . me*: do as I shall tell you.

255 *watch*: keep guard (as Cassio will be doing).
for . . . you: I'll give you your instructions.
258 *tainting*: disparaging.

260 *minister*: provide.

262 *sudden*: quick to act.
in choler: when he's angry.
haply: perhaps.

265–6 *whose . . . again*: who will not be pacified.
266 *displanting*: dismissal.

268 *prefer*: promote.

272 *warrant*: promise.
273 *his necessaries*: Othello's luggage.

Roderigo
I cannot believe that in her; she's full of most bles
condition.

Iago
Blest fig's end! The wine she drinks is made of grapes. I
she had been blest she would never have loved th
245 Moor. Blest pudding! Didst thou not see her paddl
with the palm of his hand? Didst not mark that?

Roderigo
Yes, that I did; but that was but courtesy.

Iago
Lechery, by this hand: an index and obscure prologue to
the history of lust and foul thoughts. They met so nea
250 with their lips that their breaths embraced together—
villainous thoughts, Roderigo! When these mutualitie
so marshal the way, hard at hand comes the master and
main exercise, the incorporate conclusion. Pish! But, sir
be you ruled by me. I have brought you from Venice
255 watch you tonight; for the command, I'll lay't upon you
Cassio knows you not; I'll not be far from you. Do yo
find some occasion to anger Cassio, either by speaking
too loud or tainting his discipline, or from what othe
course you please, which the time shall more favourably
260 minister.

Roderigo
Well.

Iago
Sir, he's rash and very sudden in choler, and haply with
his truncheon may strike at you: provoke him that he
may; for even out of that will I cause these of Cyprus to
265 mutiny, whose qualification shall come into no true
taste again but by the displanting of Cassio. So shall you
have a shorter journey to your desires by the means I
shall then have to prefer them, and the impediment
most profitably removed without the which there were
270 no expectation of our prosperity.

Roderigo
I will do this, if you can bring it to any opportunity.

Iago
I warrant thee. Meet me by and by at the citadel. I must
fetch his necessaries ashore. Farewell.

276 *apt . . . credit*: likely and most believable.
277 *howbeit*: although.

281 *absolute*: pure.
peradventure: perhaps.
282 *accountant*: accountable.
283 *diet*: feed.
284 *lusty*: lustful.
285 *leap'd . . . seat*: had sex with Emilia.
286 *mineral*: drug.
inwards: guts.

288 *am even'd*: get even.

292 *trash*: rubbish.
292–3 *trace . . . hunting*: follow after (like a hound) for his keen pursuit.
293 *stand . . . on*: continues to do what I want.
294 *on the hip*: at my mercy.
295 *Abuse*: slander.
rank garb: lascivious manner.
298 *egregiously*: extraordinarily.
299 *practising upon*: plotting against.

Act 2 Scene 2
The Herald reads Othello's proclamation of a public holiday until evening.

2 *certain*: reliable.
3 *mere perdition*: total destruction.
4 *triumph*: public festivity.

Roderigo
Adieu   [*Exit*
Iago
275 That Cassio loves her, I do well believe't;
That she loves him, 'tis apt and of great credit.
The Moor, howbeit that I endure him not,
Is of a constant, loving, noble nature;
And I dare think he'll prove to Desdemona
280 A most dear husband. Now, I do love her too,
Not out of absolute lust—though peradventure
I stand accountant for as great a sin—
But partly led to diet my revenge,
For that I do suspect the lusty Moor
285 Hath leap'd into my seat, the thought whereof
Doth like a poisonous mineral gnaw my inwards;
And nothing can or shall content my soul
Till I am even'd with him, wife for wife;
Or failing so, yet that I put the Moor
290 At least into a jealousy so strong
That judgement cannot cure. Which thing to do,
If this poor trash of Venice, whom I trace
For his quick hunting, stand the putting on,
I'll have our Michael Cassio on the hip,
295 Abuse him to the Moor in the rank garb—
For I fear Cassio with my night-cap too—
Make the Moor thank me, love me, and reward me,
For making him egregiously an ass,
And practising upon his peace and quiet
300 Even to madness. 'Tis here, but yet confus'd;
Knavery's plain face is never seen till us'd.   [*Exit*

SCENE 2

A public place in the town: enter Othello's Herald
with a proclamation

Herald
It is Othello's pleasure, our noble and valiant general,
that upon certain tidings now arrived importing the
mere perdition of the Turkish fleet, every man put
himself into triumph: some to dance, some to make

6 *addiction*: inclination.

8 *offices*: catering places (providing food and drink).
10 *bell*: curfew bell.
   told: struck, counted.

Act 2 Scene 3
Iago encourages Cassio to drink until, provoked by Roderigo, he becomes quarrelsome. Othello dismisses him from his office, but Iago advises him to seek Desdemona's assistance. Roderigo threatens to return to Venice.

1 *Michael*: Othello shows unusual familiarity in this use of Cassio's first name.
2 *stop*: restraint.
3 *out-sport discretion*: celebrate excessively.

6 *honest*: reliable; this word accumulates meanings as it is applied to Iago.
7 *with your earliest*: at your earliest convenience.
9–10 *The . . . you*: i.e. our marriage has yet to be consummated.

13 *Not this hour*: not for another hour.
14 *cast*: dismissed.

16 *sport for Jove*: The king of the gods was renowned for his sexual adventures.

5 bonfires, each man to what sport and revels his addiction leads him; for besides these beneficial news, it is the celebration of his nuptial. So much was his pleasure should be proclaimed. All offices are open, and there is full liberty of feasting from this present hour of
10 five till the bell have told eleven. Heaven bless the isle of Cyprus and our noble general Othello!   [*Exit*

Scene 3

Outside the guard room: enter Othello, Desdemona, Cassio, *and* Attendants

Othello
Good Michael, look you to the guard tonight.
Let's teach ourselves that honourable stop,
Not to out-sport discretion.
        Cassio
Iago hath direction what to do;
5 But notwithstanding with my personal eye
Will I look to't.
        Othello
                        Iago is most honest.
Michael, good night; tomorrow with your earliest
Let me have speech with you—Come, my dear love,
The purchase made, the fruits are to ensue;
10 That profit's yet to come 'tween me and you.
Good night.
                [*Exeunt* Othello, Desdemona, *and* Attendants

Enter Iago

Cassio
Welcome, Iago; we must to the watch.
        Iago
Not this hour, lieutenant; 'tis not yet ten o'th'clock. Our general cast us thus early for the love of his Desdemona;
15 who let us not therefore blame: he hath not yet made wanton the night with her, and she is sport for Jove.
        Cassio
She's a most exquisite lady.

'What an eye she has! Methinks it sounds a parley to provocation' (2, 3, 20–1). Richard McCabe as Iago and Henry Ian Cusick as Cassio, Royal Shakespeare Company, 2000.

18 *full of game*: sexually very active.

Iago
And I'll warrant her full of game.
    Cassio
Indeed she is a most fresh and delicate creature.
    Iago

20 *sounds a parley*: sends out a (military) summons.

20 What an eye she has! Methinks it sounds a parley to provocation.
    Cassio
An inviting eye, and yet methinks right modest.
    Iago

23 *alarum*: call to arms.

And when she speaks, is it not an alarum to love?
    Cassio
She is indeed perfection.
    Iago

25 Well, happiness to their sheets! Come, lieutenant, I have

26 *stoup*: jug.
here without: just outside.
brace: pair.
27 *gallants*: good chaps.
fain: like to.
have a measure: drink a toast.
29–30 *poor . . . brains*: a very poor head (i.e. he is quickly intoxicated).

a stoup of wine, and here without are a brace of Cyprus gallants, that would fain have a measure to the health of the black Othello.
    Cassio
Not tonight, good Iago; I have very poor and unhappy

30 brains for drinking. I could well wish courtesy would invent some other custom of entertainment.
    Iago

32 *I'll . . . you*: I'll drink in your place.

O, they are our friends—but one cup; I'll drink for you.
    Cassio
I have drunk but one cup tonight, and that was craftily

33–4 *craftily qualified*: carefully diluted.
34 *innovation*: disturbance.
35 *here*: in my head.

qualified too; and behold what innovation it makes

35 here. I am unfortunate in the infirmity and dare not task my weakness with any more.
    Iago
What, man! 'Tis a night of revels; the gallants desire it.
    Cassio
Where are they?
    Iago
Here at the door; I pray you call them in.
    Cassio

40 *it dislikes me*: I don't like it.

40 I'll do't, but it dislikes me.   [*Exit*
    Iago

41 *fasten . . . him*: get him to have just one more drink; Iago moves into verse for this moment of self-revelation.

If I can fasten but one cup upon him,
With that which he hath drunk tonight already,

43 *full . . . offence*: ready to take and
give offence.
44 *my . . . dog*: any girl's pet dog.
sick: love-sick.

He'll be as full of quarrel and offence
As my young mistress' dog. Now my sick fool
   Roderigo,
45 Whom love hath turn'd almost the wrong side out,
To Desdemona hath tonight carous'd

47 *Potations pottle-deep*: whole tankards
full of drink.
48 *swelling*: arrogant.
49 *hold . . . distance*: are jealously
protective of their honours.
50 *very elements*: characteristic types.
51 *fluster'd*: excited, made drunk.
52 *watch*: are awake.

Potations pottle-deep, and he's to watch.
Three lads of Cyprus, noble swelling spirits,
That hold their honours in a wary distance,
50 The very elements of this warlike isle,
Have I tonight fluster'd with flowing cups;
And they watch too. Now, 'mongst this flock of
   drunkards,

53 *put . . . action*: incite Cassio to some
quarrel.

Am I to put our Cassio in some action
That may offend the isle. But here they come.

   Enter Cassio, Montano, *and* Gentlemen

55 *consequence*: what happens next.
approve: confirm.
56 *My . . . stream*: everything is going
well.
57 *rouse*: large quantity of drink.

55 If consequence do but approve my dream,
My boat sails freely, both with wind and stream.
   Cassio
'Fore God, they have given me a rouse already.
   Montano

58 *past a pint*: more than a pint.

Good faith, a little one; not past a pint, as I am a soldier.
   Iago
Some wine, ho!
   [*Sings*]

60 *cannikin*: small drinking-can.

60   And let me the cannikin clink, clink,
   And let me the cannikin clink;
     A soldier's a man,
     O, man's life's but a span,
   Why then, let a soldier drink.

63 *man's . . . span*: 'Thou hast made my
days as it were a span long' (Psalm
39:6); 'span' = short extent.

65 Some wine, boys.
   Cassio
'Fore God, an excellent song.
   Iago
I learned it in England, where indeed they are most
potent in potting. Your Dane, your German, and your

68 *potent in potting*: heavy drinkers.
69 *swag-bellied*: having a sagging belly.

swag-bellied Hollander—drink, ho!—are nothing to
70 your English.
   Cassio
Is your Englishman so exquisite in his drinking?

72 *with facility*: easily.

73 *sweats not*: finds it no effort.
    Almain: German.

73–4 *gives . . . vomit*: makes a Dutchman
    sick.
    pottle: tankard.

76 *do you justice*: match your pledge.

78 *and*: The extra syllable helps the
    metre.
79 *crown*: The coin was stamped with a
    crown.
80 *held*: thought.
81 *lown*: rascal, rogue.

84 *pride*: extravagance.
85 *auld*: old.

94 *quality*: rank.

Iago

Why, he drinks you with facility your Dane dead drunk
he sweats not to overthrow your Almain; he gives you
Hollander a vomit ere the next pottle can be filled.

Cassio

75 To the health of our general!

Montano

I am for it, lieutenant, and I'll do you justice.

Iago

O sweet England!

[*Sings*]

King Stephen was and a worthy peer,
    His breeches cost him but a crown;
80 He held them sixpence all too dear,
    With that he call'd the tailor lown.

He was a wight of high renown,
    And thou art but of low degree;
'Tis pride that pulls the country down;
85   Then take thine auld cloak about thee.

Some wine, ho!

Cassio

'Fore God, this is a more exquisite song than the other.

Iago

Will you hear't again?

Cassio

No, for I hold him to be unworthy of his place that does
90 those things. Well, God's above all, and there be souls
must be saved, and there be souls must not be saved.

Iago

It's true, good lieutenant.

Cassio

For mine own part—no offence to the general, nor any
man of quality—I hope to be saved.

Iago

95 And so do I too, lieutenant.

Cassio

Ay, but by your leave, not before me; the lieutenant is to
be saved before the ancient. Let's have no more of this;
let's to our affairs. God forgive us our sins! Gentlemen,
let's look to our business. Do not think, gentlemen, I am

100 drunk; this is my ancient, this is my right hand, and this
is my left hand. I am not drunk now, I can stand well
enough, and I speak well enough.

All
Excellent well.

Cassio
Why, very well then; you must not think then that I am
105 drunk.   [*Exit*

Montano
To the platform, masters. Come, let's set the watch.

Iago
You see this fellow that is gone before,
He is a soldier fit to stand by Caesar
And give direction. And do but see his vice—
110 'Tis to his virtue a just equinox,
The one as long as th'other. 'Tis pity of him.
I fear the trust Othello puts him in,
On some odd time of his infirmity,
Will shake this island.

Montano
                                      But is he often thus?

Iago
115 'Tis evermore the prologue to his sleep:
He'll watch the horologe a double set,
If drink rock not his cradle.

Montano
                                      It were well
The general were put in mind of it.
Perhaps he sees it not, or his good nature
120 Prizes the virtue that appears in Cassio
And looks not on his evils: is not this true?

Enter Roderigo

Iago
[*Aside to* Roderigo] How now, Roderigo?
I pray you after the lieutenant, go.   [*Exit* Roderigo

Montano
And 'tis great pity that the noble Moor
125 Should hazard such a place as his own second
With one of an ingraft infirmity;

---

106 *platform*: gun rampart.
    set the watch: mount the guard.

108 *stand by*: be the equal of.

110 *just equinox*: exact equivalent.

113 *odd time*: chance moment.
114 *shake*: destroy.

115 *'Tis . . . sleep*: he's always like this
    before going to sleep.
116 *watch . . . set*: stay awake for a couple
    of revolutions of the clock.

125 *hazard . . . second*: risk giving the
    position of lieutenant.
126 *ingraft*: deeply rooted.

It were an honest action to say so
To the Moor.
   Iago
                 Not I, for this fair island:
I do love Cassio well, and would do much
130 To cure him of this evil.

   A cry of 'Help, help!' within

                         But hark! what noise?

   Enter Cassio, *pursuing* Roderigo

   Cassio
Zounds, you rogue, you rascal!
   Montano
What's the matter, lieutenant?
   Cassio
A knave teach me my duty! I'll beat the knave into a
twiggen bottle.
   Roderigo
135 Beat me?
   Cassio
Dost thou prate, rogue?

   He strikes Roderigo

   Montano
Nay, good lieutenant, I pray you, sir, hold your hand.
   Cassio
Let me go, sir; or I'll knock you o'er the mazzard.
   Montano
Come, come, you're drunk.
   Cassio
140 Drunk?

   They fight

   Iago
[*Aside to* Roderigo] Away I say, go out and cry a
mutiny.   [*Exit* Roderigo

134 *twiggen bottle*: bottle covered with
wickerwork; perhaps Cassio threatens
to slash Roderigo with his sword.

138 *mazzard*: head, skull.

141 *mutiny*: riot.

Nay, good lieutenant; God's will, gentlemen!
Help ho! Lieutenant, sir! Montano, sir!
Help, masters, here's a goodly watch indeed!

A bell rings

145 Who's that which rings the bell? Diabolo, ho!
The town will rise. God's will, lieutenant, hold!
You will be sham'd forever.

Enter Othello, *and* Gentlemen *with weapons*

Othello
What is the matter here?
Montano
                           Zounds, I bleed still.
I am hurt to th'death.
Othello
                           Hold for your lives!
Iago
150 Hold ho, lieutenant, sir; Montano, gentlemen,
Have you forgot all place of sense and duty?
Hold! the general speaks to you; hold, for shame!
Othello
Why, how now, ho! From whence ariseth this?
Are we turn'd Turks, and to ourselves do that
155 Which heaven hath forbid the Ottomites?
For Christian shame, put by this barbarous brawl.
He that stirs next to carve for his own rage
Holds his soul light: he dies upon his motion.
Silence that dreadful bell: it frights the isle
160 From her propriety. What is the matter, masters?
Honest Iago, that looks dead with grieving,
Speak. Who began this? On thy love, I charge thee.
Iago
I do not know. Friends all but now, even now,
In quarter and in terms like bride and groom,
165 Divesting them for bed; and then but now—
As if some planet had unwitted men—
Swords out and tilting one at other's breasts
In opposition bloody. I cannot speak

145 *Diabolo*: the devil (Spanish).
146 *rise*: grow riotous.

151 *place*: dignity.

154 *do that*: i.e. slaughter our own soldiers.
155 *forbid*: denied (by sending the storm).

157 *to carve . . . rage*: to stab someone in anger.
158 *Holds . . . light*: sets little value on his life.
160 *propriety*: normal peaceful state.

162 *love*: loyalty.

163 *even now*: only just now.
164 *quarter*: conduct.
165 *Divesting*: undressing.
166 *unwitted men*: driven men out of their minds; planets were thought to have powerful influence over the human mind.
167 *tilting*: striking.
168 *speak*: explain.

169 *peevish odds*: senseless quarrel.

170 *would*: I would rather.

171 *to*: to be.

172 *are . . . forgot*: have forgotten yourself like this.

174 *civil*: law-abiding.

175 *stillness*: sober behaviour.

177 *censure*: judgement.

178 *unlace*: loosen (like purse strings).

181 *hurt to danger*: seriously injured.

183 *something . . . me*: is rather painful for me.

186 *self-charity*: self-protection.

189 *safer guides*: reason.

190 *collied*: blackened.

194 *rout*: uproar.

195 *approv'd*: found guilty.

197 *town of*: town garrisoned for.

199 *manage*: conduct.

200 *court . . . safety*: in the very guardroom.

Any beginning to this peevish odds:
170 And would in action glorious I had lost
Those legs that brought me to a part of it.
    Othello
How comes it, Michael, you are thus forgot?
    Cassio
I pray you pardon me, I cannot speak.
    Othello
Worthy Montano, you were wont be civil:
175 The gravity and stillness of your youth
The world hath noted; and your name is great
In mouths of wisest censure. What's the matter
That you unlace your reputation thus,
And spend your rich opinion for the name
180 Of a night-brawler? Give me answer to it.
    Montano
Worthy Othello, I am hurt to danger;
Your officer Iago can inform you—
While I spare speech, which something now offends
    me—
Of all that I do know; nor know I aught
185 By me that's said or done amiss this night,
Unless self-charity be sometimes a vice,
And to defend ourselves it be a sin
When violence assails us.
    Othello
                  Now by heaven
My blood begins my safer guides to rule,
190 And passion having my best judgement collied,
Assays to lead the way. Zounds, if I stir,
Or do but lift this arm, the best of you
Shall sink in my rebuke. Give me to know
How this foul rout began, who set it on,
195 And he that is approv'd in this offence,
Though he had twinn'd with me, both at a birth,
Shall lose me. What, in a town of war,
Yet wild, the people's hearts brimful of fear,
To manage private and domestic quarrel,
200 In night, and on the court and guard of safety?
'Tis monstrous. Iago, who began't?

Montano

If partially affin'd or leagued in office,
Thou dost deliver more or less than truth,
Thou art no soldier.

Iago

                                        Touch me not so near.
205 I had rather have this tongue cut from my mouth
Than it should do offence to Michael Cassio.
Yet, I persuade myself, to speak the truth
Shall nothing wrong him. This it is, general:
Montano and myself being in speech,
210 There comes a fellow crying out for help,
And Cassio following him with determin'd sword
To execute upon him. Sir, this gentleman
Steps in to Cassio and entreats his pause;
Myself the crying fellow did pursue,
215 Lest by his clamour—as it so fell out—
The town might fall in fright. He, swift of foot,
Outran my purpose and I return'd the rather
For that I heard the clink and fall of swords
And Cassio high in oath, which till tonight
220 I ne'er might say before. When I came back—
For this was brief—I found them close together
At blow and thrust, even as again they were
When you yourself did part them.
More of this matter can I not report;
225 But men are men; the best sometimes forget.
Though Cassio did some little wrong to him,
As men in rage strike those that wish them best,
Yet surely Cassio, I believe, receiv'd
From him that fled some strange indignity
230 Which patience could not pass.

Othello

                                        I know, Iago,
Thy honesty and love doth mince this matter,
Making it light to Cassio. Cassio, I love thee,
But never more be officer of mine.

Enter Desdemona *attended*

---

202 *partially affin'd*: leaning to any side.
leagued in office: showing loyalty to a colleague.

211 *determin'd*: drawn.

212 *To . . . him*: to strike him.
this gentleman: i.e. Montano.

213 *Steps in*: goes up to.
entreats his pause: begs him to stop.

217 *Outran . . . purpose*: ran faster than I thought.
the rather: all the sooner.

219 *high in oath*: swearing loudly.

221 *close*: fighting.

229 *indignity*: insult.

230 *pass*: ignore.

231 *mince*: tone down.

232 *Making . . . Cassio*: making light of Cassio's part in the fight.

Look if my gentle love be not rais'd up!

235 I'll make thee an example.

Desdemona

What's the matter, dear?

Othello

All's well now, sweeting; come away to bed.

Sir, for your hurts myself will be your surgeon.

[*Montano is led off*

Iago, look with care about the town,

And silence those whom this vile brawl distracted.

240 Come, Desdemona, 'tis the soldier's life

To have their balmy slumbers wak'd with strife.

[*Exeunt all but* Iago *and* Cassio

Iago

What, are you hurt, lieutenant?

Cassio

Ay, past all surgery.

Iago

Marry, God forbid!

Cassio

245 Reputation, reputation, reputation! O, I have lost my
reputation! I have lost the immortal part of myself, and
what remains is bestial. My reputation, Iago, my
reputation!

Iago

As I am an honest man, I thought you had received

250 some bodily wound: there is more of sense in that than
in reputation. Reputation is an idle and most false
imposition, oft got without merit and lost without
deserving. You have lost no reputation at all, unless you
repute yourself such a loser. What, man! There are ways

255 to recover the general again. You are but now cast in his
mood, a punishment more in policy that in malice, even
so as one would beat his offenceless dog to affright an
imperious lion. Sue to him again, and he's yours.

Cassio

I will rather sue to be despised than to deceive so good a

260 commander with so light, so drunken, and so indiscreet
an officer. Drunk! And speak parrot! And squabble!
Swagger! Swear! And discourse fustian with one's own

---

237 *myself . . . surgeon*: I'll pay your medical expenses.

243 *past all surgery*: beyond medical help; the change from verse to prose signals a change in the mood and pace of the scene.

250 *of sense*: of physical feeling.
251–4 *Reputation . . . loser*: Compare Iago's contrary opinion in 3, 3, 156–62.

254 *repute*: consider.
255 *recover the general*: win back Othello's friendship.
255–6 *You . . . mood*: you have only been dismissed because of his temper.
256 *in policy*: for political reasons.
  malice: ill-will.
257–8 *beat . . . lion*: punish an innocent unimportant creature in order to deter a powerful and dangerous one.
258 *Sue*: appeal.
261 *speak parrot*: talk nonsense.
262 *fustian*: rubbish.

shadow! O thou invisible spirit of wine, if thou hast no name to be known by, let us call thee devil!

Iago

265 What was he that you followed with your sword? What had he done to you?

Cassio

I know not.

Iago

Is't possible?

Cassio

I remember a mass of things, but nothing distinctly: a 270 quarrel, but nothing wherefore. O God, that men should put an enemy in their mouths to steal away their brains! That we should with joy, pleasance, revel, and applause transform ourselves into beasts!

Iago

Why, but you are now well enough. How came you thus 275 recovered?

Cassio

It hath pleased the devil drunkenness to give place to the devil wrath; one unperfectness shows me another, to make me frankly despise myself.

Iago

Come, you are too severe a moraler. As the time, the 280 place, and the condition of this country stands, I could heartily wish this had not befallen; but since it is as it is, mend it for your own good.

Cassio

I will ask him for my place again; he shall tell me I am a drunkard. Had I as many mouths as Hydra, such an 285 answer would stop them all. To be now a sensible man, by and by a fool, and presently a beast! O strange! Every inordinate cup is unblessed, and the ingredience is a devil.

Iago

Come, come, good wine is a good familiar creature, if it 290 be well used; exclaim no more against it. And, good lieutenant, I think you think I love you.

Cassio

I have well approved it, sir. I drunk!

---

270 *nothing wherefore*: not what it was about.

272 *pleasance*: pleasure.

273 *applause*: i.e. the desire for applause.

277 *unperfectness*: imperfection.

278 *frankly*: completely.

279 *moraler*: moralist.

281 *heartily*: with all my heart.
befallen: happened like this.

284 *Hydra*: In classical mythology, this was a snake with many heads; it was killed by Hercules.

285 *stop*: silence.
now: at one moment.
sensible: Here the word has its modern meaning.

286 *by and by*: very soon.
presently: now.

286–7 *Every inordinate cup*: every drink too many.

287 *unblessed*: cursed.
ingredience: contents.

289 *familiar creature*: friendly spirit (with perhaps a play on 'familiar' = a witch's personal devil-servant).

290 *exclaim . . . it*: stop grumbling at it.

292 *approved it*: put it to the test.

293 *at a time*: at some time.

297 *mark*: observation.
     parts: qualities.
298–9 *put you . . . again*: get your job
     back.
299 *free*: generous.

303 *splinter*: mend (by putting on a
     splint).
     lay: bet.
304–5 *this crack . . . before*: i.e. as a
     mended bone is said to be stronger
     than before it was broken.

308 *I think it freely*: I well believe it.
     betimes: early.
309 *undertake*: take up the matter.
310 *check*: stop.

316 *Probal*: reasonable.
318 *inclining*: sympathetic.
     subdue: persuade.
319 *fram'd as fruitful*: naturally as
     generous.
320 *free elements*: unrestrained natural
     forces.
321 *win*: persuade.
     his baptism: i.e. his Christian faith.
322 *seals . . . sin*: Christian tokens (such
     as the sign of the cross) of redemption
     from sin.
     redeemed: redeemèd.
323 *enfetter'd to*: bound by.
324 *list*: wishes.
325 *her appetite*: his sexual desire for her.
326 *function*: will.

Iago
You or any man living may be drunk at a time, man. I'll
tell you what you shall do. Our general's wife is now the
295 general. I may say so in this respect, for that he hath
devoted and given up himself to the contemplation,
mark, and denotement of her parts and graces. Confess
yourself freely to her, importune her help to put you in
your place again. She is of so free, so kind, so apt, so
300 blest a disposition, that she holds it a vice in her
goodness not to do more than she is requested. This
broken joint between you and her husband entreat her
to splinter; and my fortunes against any lay worth
naming, this crack of your love shall grow stronger than
305 it was before.

Cassio
You advise me well.

Iago
I protest, in the sincerity of love and honest kindness.

Cassio
I think it freely; and betimes in the morning I will
beseech the virtuous Desdemona to undertake for me. I
310 am desperate of my fortunes if they check me here.

Iago
You are in the right. Good night, lieutenant, I must to
the watch.

Cassio
Good night, honest Iago.   [*Exit*

Iago
And what's he then that says I play the villain,
315 When this advice is free I give, and honest,
Probal to thinking, and indeed the course
To win the Moor again? For 'tis most easy
Th'inclining Desdemona to subdue
In any honest suit. She's fram'd as fruitful
320 As the free elements; and then for her
To win the Moor, were't to renounce his baptism,
All seals and symbols of redeemed sin,
His soul is so enfetter'd to her love,
That she may make, unmake, do what she list,
325 Even as her appetite shall play the god
With his weak function. How am I then a villain

To counsel Cassio to this parallel course
Directly to his good? Divinity of hell!
When devils will the blackest sins put on,
330 They do suggest at first with heavenly shows
As I do now. For whiles this honest fool
Plies Desdemona to repair his fortunes,
And she for him pleads strongly to the Moor,
I'll pour this pestilence into his ear:
335 That she repeals him for her body's lust;
And by how much she strives to do him good,
She shall undo her credit with the Moor.
So will I turn her virtue into pitch,
And out of her own goodness make the net
340 That shall enmesh them all.

Enter Roderigo

How now, Roderigo?
Roderigo
I do follow here in the chase, not like a hound that
hunts, but one that fills up the cry. My money is almost
spent; I have been tonight exceedingly well cudgelled;
and I think the issue will be, I shall have so much
345 experience for my pains; and so, with no money at all,
and a little more wit, return again to Venice.
Iago
How poor are they that have no patience!
What wound did ever heal but by degrees?
Thou know'st we work by wit and not by witchcraft,
350 And wit depends on dilatory time.
Does't not go well? Cassio hath beaten thee,
And thou by that small hurt hath cashier'd Cassio.
Though other things grow fair against the sun,
Yet fruits that blossom first will first be ripe.
355 Content thyself awhile. By th'mass, 'tis morning:
Pleasure and action make the hours seem short.
Retire thee, go where thou art billeted.
Away, I say, thou shalt know more hereafter—
Nay, get thee gone.   [*Exit* Roderigo
Two things are to be done.
360 My wife must move for Cassio to her mistress—

327 *parallel*: i.e. to Iago's plot.
328 *Divinity*: theology.
329 *put on*: encourage.
330 *suggest*: tempt.

332 *Plies*: pleads with.

335 *repeals*: wants to have him reinstated.

338 *pitch*: a black sticky substance
defiling all it touches.

342 *fills . . . cry*: makes one of the pack.

346 *wit*: sense.

349 *wit*: cunning.
350 *dilatory*: dawdling.

352 *cashier'd Cassio*: got Cassio
dismissed.
353–4 *Though . . . ripe*: Another of Iago's
cryptic remarks: most things grow well
in the sunshine, but the fruits that are
the first to blossom are also the
earliest to ripen. Cassio's dismissal is
the first sign of success—the
'blossom'—for Roderigo.
355 *'tis morning*: The time has passed
quickly; it was not ten o'clock at night
when the scene started (line 13).
358 *hereafter*: later.
360 *move*: plead.

362 *the while*: meanwhile.
 apart: aside.
363 *jump*: at the precise moment.
364 *Soliciting*: asking favours.
365 *device*: scheme.

I'll set her on.
Myself the while to draw the Moor apart,
And bring him jump when he may Cassio find
Soliciting his wife. Ay, that's the way:

365 Dull not device by coldness and delay.   [*Exit*

ACT 3

Act 3 Scene 1
Cassio asks Emilia to help him gain access
to Desdemona.

1 *Masters, play here*: It was customary
to wake the newly married couple with
music after their first night together.
content your pains: pay you for your
trouble.

3–4 *in Naples . . . nose*: The Neapolitan
accent may have been rather nasal in
sound; and the Clown is attempting
some poor sexual joke based on the
'Neapolitan disease', which was a
venereal condition.
5 *How . . . how?*: what do you mean?
6 *wind instruments*: probably a form of
bagpipe (see line 19).

7 *Ay, marry*: yes indeed.
8 *thereby . . . tail*: A proverbial
phrase—but the Clown makes a pun
on 'tail' (= penis) and 'wind
instrument' (= anus).

15 *may not*: cannot.
to't again: play on.

SCENE 1

Outside Desdemona*'s bedchamber: enter* Cassio,
Musicians, *and* Clown

Cassio
Masters, play here; I will content your pains.
Something that's brief, and bid 'Good morrow,
   general.'

They play

Clown
Why, masters, have your instruments been in Naples,
that they speak i'th'nose thus?
First Musician
5 How, sir, how?
Clown
Are these, I pray you, wind instruments?
First Musician
Ay, marry are they, sir.
Clown
O, thereby hangs a tail.
First Musician
Whereby hangs a tale, sir?
Clown
10 Marry, sir, by many a wind instrument that I know. But,
masters, here's money for you; and the general so likes
your music that he desires you, for love's sake, to make
no more noise with it.
First Musician
Well, sir, we will not.
Clown
15 If you have any music that may not be heard, to't again;
but, as they say, to hear music the general does not
greatly care.

First Musician

We have none such, sir.

  Clown

Then put up your pipes in your bag, for I'll away. Go,

20 vanish into air, away!   [*Exeunt* Musicians

  Cassio

Dost thou hear, mine honest friend?

  Clown

No, I hear not your honest friend; I hear you.

  Cassio

Prithee keep up thy quillets—there's a poor piece of
gold for thee. If the gentlewoman that attends the
25 general's wife be stirring, tell her there's one Cassio
entreats her a little favour of speech. Wilt thou do this?

  Clown

She is stirring, sir; if she will stir hither, I shall seem to
notify unto her.

  Cassio

Do, good my friend.   [*Exit* Clown

Enter Iago

     In happy time, Iago.

  Iago

30 You have not been abed then?

  Cassio

Why, no; the day had broke before we parted.
I have made bold, Iago,
To send in to your wife. My suit to her
Is that she will to virtuous Desdemona
35 Procure me some access.

  Iago

     I'll send her to you presently;
And I'll devise a mean to draw the Moor
Out of the way, that your converse and business
May be more free.

  Cassio

    I humbly thank you for't.

       [*Exit* Iago

I never knew a Florentine more kind and honest.

Enter Emilia

---

23 *quillets*: quibbles.

25 *stirring*: awake.

27 *stirring*: sexually active.
27–8 *seem . . . her*: The Clown is making
 fun of Cassio's courtly manners.

29 *In happy time*: You have come at the
 right time.

30 *abed*: to bed.

33 *suit*: request.

35 *presently*: immediately.
36 *a mean*: a way.

39 *a Florentine*: i.e. one of my own
 countrymen (Iago is a Venetian).

Emilia

40 Good morrow, good lieutenant; I am sorry
For your displeasure; but all will sure be well.
The general and his wife are talking of it,
And she speaks for you stoutly. The Moor replies
That he you hurt is of great fame in Cyprus
45 And great affinity, and that in wholesome wisdom
He might not but refuse you; but he protests he loves
    you,
And needs no other suitor but his likings
To take the safest occasion by the front
To bring you in again.
    Cassio
                        Yet I beseech you,
50 If you think fit, or that it may be done,
Give me advantage of some brief discourse
With Desdemon alone.
    Emilia
                        Pray you, come in;
I will bestow you where you shall have time
To speak your bosom freely.
    Cassio
                       I am much bound to you.
                                  [Exeunt

SCENE 2

Othello's headquarters: enter Othello, Iago, *and* Gentlemen

Othello
These letters give, Iago, to the pilot,
And by him do my duties to the senate.
That done, I will be walking on the works;
Repair there to me.
    Iago
                    Well, my good lord, I'll do't.   *[Exit*
    Othello
5 This fortification, gentlemen, shall we see't?
    Gentlemen
We'll wait upon your lordship.   *[Exeunt*

Notes (left column):

41 *your displeasure*: that you have incurred Othello's displeasure.

43 *stoutly*: loyally.

44 *of great fame*: well known.

45 *great affinity*: with important connections.
wholesome wisdom: all commonsense.
46 *refuse*: dismiss.

48 *take . . . front*: take the first convenient opportunity; opportunity must be seized by the forelock, being (as depicted emblematically) bald behind.
49 *in again*: back in favour.

54 *bosom*: heart.
much bound: very grateful.

Act 3 Scene 2
Othello sends letters to Venice.

1 *pilot*: i.e. of the ship returning to Venice.
2 *do my duties*: pay my respects.
3 *works*: fortifications.
4 *Repair*: return.

Act 3 Scene 3
Iago sows suspicion in Othello's mind until the Moor is convinced that his wife is no longer true to him. Emilia gives Desdemona's handkerchief to her husband.

SCENE 3

Othello's lodgings: enter Desdemona, Cassio, *and* Emilia

Desdemona
Be thou assur'd, good Cassio, I will do
All my abilities in thy behalf.
    Emilia
Good madam, do; I warrant it grieves my husband
As if the case were his.
    Desdemona
5 O, that's an honest fellow. Do not doubt, Cassio,
But I will have my lord and you again
As friendly as you were.
    Cassio
                      Bounteous madam,
Whatever shall become of Michael Cassio,
He's never anything but your true servant.
    Desdemona
10 I know't; I thank you. You do love my lord,
You have known him long, and be you well assur'd
He shall in strangeness stand no farther off
Than in a politic distance.
    Cassio
                     Ay, but, lady,
That policy may either last so long
15 Or feed upon such nice and waterish diet,
Or breed itself so out of circumstance,
That I being absent and my place supplied,
My general will forget my love and service.
    Desdemona
Do not doubt that. Before Emilia here,
20 I give thee warrant of thy place. Assure thee
If I do vow a friendship, I'll perform it
To the last article. My lord shall never rest,
I'll watch him tame and talk him out of patience;
His bed shall seem a school, his board a shrift;
25 I'll intermingle every thing he does
With Cassio's suit. Therefore be merry, Cassio;

12 *strangeness*: estrangement.
13 *politic*: politically necessary.

15 *nice*: thin, meagre.
16 *breed . . . circumstance*: produce so few opportunities.
17 *supplied*: taken by someone else.

19 *doubt*: fear.
    Before: in the presence of.
20 *warrant*: guarantee.

22 *article*: (legal) detail.

23 *watch him*: keep him awake (a technique for taming hawks).
24 *board . . . shrift*: mealtime table seem like a confessional.

27 *solicitor*: advocate.

28 *give . . . away*: abandon your case.

Thy solicitor shall rather die
Than give thy cause away.

Enter Othello *and* Iago

Emilia
Madam, here comes my lord.
Cassio
30 Madam, I'll take my leave.
Desdemona
Why, stay and hear me speak.
Cassio
Madam, not now: I am very ill at ease,
Unfit for mine own purposes.
Desdemona

34 *your discretion*: as you think best.

Well, do your discretion.   [*Exit* Cassio
Iago

35 *I like not that*: Iago begins his
campaign.

35 Ha! I like not that.
Othello
                              What dost thou say?
Iago
Nothing, my lord; or if—I know not what.
Othello
Was not that Cassio parted from my wife?
Iago
Cassio, my lord? No, sure I cannot think it
That he would steal away so guilty-like,
40 Seeing you coming.
Othello
                              I do believe 'twas he.
Desdemona
How now, my lord?
I have been talking with a suitor here,
A man that languishes in your displeasure.
Othello
Who is't you mean?
Desdemona
45 Why, your lieutenant, Cassio. Good my lord,
If I have any grace or power to move you,

47 *His . . . take*: make peace with him
now.

His present reconciliation take.
For if he be not one that truly loves you,

49 *in cunning*: deliberately.

58 *dinner*: the meal eaten at mid-day.

64 *in . . . reason*: by normal standards.

65–6 *example . . . best*: even the highest officers must be made an example to the other soldiers; see *2, 3, 235*.

66–7 *is not . . . check*: is hardly worth a private rebuke.

70 *mammering on*: hesitating.

74 *bring him in*: i.e. back in favour.
   By'r Lady: by the Virgin Mary.

That errs in ignorance, and not in cunning,
50 I have no judgement in an honest face.
I prithee call him back.
>   **Othello**
>   Went he hence now?
Desdemona
Ay, sooth; so humbled
That he hath left part of his grief with me
To suffer with him. Good love, call him back.
>   **Othello**
55 Not now, sweet Desdemon; some other time.
>   **Desdemona**
But shall't be shortly?
>   **Othello**
>   The sooner, sweet, for you.
Desdemona
Shall't be tonight at supper?
>   **Othello**
>   No, not tonight.
Desdemona
Tomorrow dinner then?
>   **Othello**
>   I shall not dine at home.
I meet the captains at the citadel.
>   **Desdemona**
60 Why, then, tomorrow night, or Tuesday morn,
On Tuesday noon, or night; on Wednesday morn.
I prithee name the time, but let it not
Exceed three days. In faith, he's penitent;
And yet his trespass, in our common reason—
65 Save that, they say, the wars must make example
Out of their best—is not almost a fault
T'incur a private check. When shall he come?
Tell me, Othello. I wonder in my soul
What you would ask me that I should deny,
70 Or stand so mammering on. What! Michael Cassio,
That came a-wooing with you, and so many a time
When I have spoke of you dispraisingly
Hath tane your part, to have so much to do
To bring him in? By'r Lady, I could do much—

75 *will*: wishes.

76 *boon*: personal favour (for herself).
77 *as*: as if.

79 *peculiar*: personal.
   profit: benefit.

81 *touch . . . indeed*: really put your love
   to the test.
82 *poise . . . weight*: weight and serious
   implications.
83 *fearful . . . granted*: not easy to be
   decided.

84 *Whereon*: at this point.

87 *straight*: immediately.

88 *fancies*: desires.

90 *wretch*: the term is used
   affectionately.
90-1 *Perdition . . . thee*: let me be
   damned if I do not love you.
92 *Chaos is come again*: i.e. it will be the
   end of the world; the Elizabethans
   believed that at the end of the world
   all things would return to the state of
   chaos that existed before creation.

96 *But . . . thought*: I just wondered.

Othello
75 Prithee no more. Let him come when he will;
   I will deny thee nothing.
   Desdemona
                    Why, this is not a boon;
   'Tis as I should entreat you wear your gloves,
   Or feed on nourishing dishes, or keep you warm,
   Or sue to you to do a peculiar profit
80 To your own person. Nay, when I have a suit
   Wherein I mean to touch your love indeed,
   It shall be full of poise and difficult weight,
   And fearful to be granted.
   Othello
                    I will deny thee nothing.
   Whereon, I do beseech thee, grant me this,
85 To leave me but a little to myself.
   Desdemona
   Shall I deny you? No; farewell, my lord.
   Othello
   Farewell, my Desdemona, I'll come to thee straight.
   Desdemona
   Emilia, come. Be as your fancies teach you;
   Whate'er you be, I am obedient.
                    [*Exeunt* Desdemona *and* Emilia
   Othello
90 Excellent wretch! Perdition catch my soul
   But I do love thee; and when I love thee not,
   Chaos is come again.
   Iago
                    My noble lord—
   Othello
   What dost thou say, Iago?
   Iago
                    Did Michael Cassio,
   When you woo'd my lady, know of your love?
   Othello
95 He did from first to last. Why dost thou ask?
   Iago
   But for a satisfaction of my thought;
   No further harm.

Othello
                                    Why of thy thought, Iago?
　Iago
I did not think he had been acquainted with her.
　Othello
O yes, and went between us very oft.
　Iago
100 Indeed?
　Othello
Indeed? Ay, indeed. Discern'st thou aught in that?
Is he not honest?
　Iago
Honest, my lord?
　Othello
Honest? Ay, honest.
　Iago
105 My lord, for aught I know.
　Othello
                                    What dost thou think?
　Iago
Think, my lord?
　Othello
Think, my lord! By heaven, he echoes me,
As if there were some monster in his thought
Too hideous to be shown. Thou dost mean something.
110 I heard thee say even now thou lik'st not that,
When Cassio left my wife. What didst not like?
And when I told thee he was of my counsel
In my whole course of wooing, thou cried'st 'Indeed?'
And didst contract and purse thy brow together,
115 As if thou then hadst shut up in thy brain
Some horrible conceit. If thou dost love me,
Show me thy thought.
　Iago
My lord, you know I love you.
　Othello
                                    I think thou dost;
And for I know thou'rt full of love and honesty,
120 And weigh'st thy words before thou giv'st them breath,
Therefore these stops of thine fright me the more;
For such things in a false disloyal knave

99 *went between us*: i.e. carrying messages.

100 *Indeed?*: The actor playing Iago is directed how to react by Othello's description of his behaviour at line 114.

101 *Discern'st . . . that?*: Can you see anything wrong in that?

108 *monster*: see line 168 below.

112 *of my counsel*: in my confidence.

113 *course of wooing*: courtship.

114 *purse*: knit.

115 *shut up in thy brain*: you were thinking in your head.

116 *conceit*: idea.

117 *Show*: tell.

120 *weigh'st*: consider.
     giv'st them breath: speak them.

121 *stops*: hesitations.

23 *of custom*: customary.
   just: trustworthy.
24 *close dilations*: secret expressions of thought.
25 *passion . . . rule*: emotion cannot control.

28 *would . . . none*: I wish they would not seem to be honest men.

32 *speak . . . thinkings*: tell me what you really think.
33 *As thou dost ruminate*: when you really think it over.

37 *they*: i.e. his thoughts.
38 *As where's*: where, for example, is.
39 *breast*: heart.
40 *apprehensions*: ideas.
41–2 *Keep . . . lawful*: hold their local courts and sessions, and sit in judgement along with respectable ideas.
43 *conspire*: plot.
   against thy friend: i.e. against Othello himself.
44–5 *mak'st . . . thoughts*: don't tell him what you are thinking.

46 *perchance*: perhaps.
   vicious in my guess: badly misinterpreting.
47 *my nature's plague*: a characteristic fault of mine.
48 *jealousy*: suspicion.
49 *Shapes*: imagines.
50 *conceits*: understands.

Are tricks of custom; but in a man that's just,
They're close dilations, working from the heart,
125 That passion cannot rule.
    Iago
                              For Michael Cassio,
I dare be sworn I think that he is honest.
    Othello
I think so too.
    Iago
                  Men should be what they seem;
Or those that be not, would they might seem none!
    Othello
Certain, men should be what they seem.
    Iago
130 Why then, I think Cassio's an honest man.
    Othello
Nay, yet there's more in this.
I prithee speak to me as to thy thinkings,
As thou dost ruminate, and give thy worst of thoughts
The worst of words.
    Iago
                      Good my lord, pardon me;
135 Though I am bound to every act of duty,
I am not bound to that all slaves are free to.
Utter my thoughts! Why, say they are vile and false?
As where's that palace, whereinto foul things
Sometimes intrude not? Who has a breast so pure,
140 But some uncleanly apprehensions
Keep leets and law-days, and in session sit
With meditations lawful?
    Othello
Thou dost conspire against thy friend, Iago,
If thou but think'st him wrong'd, and mak'st his ear
145 A stranger to thy thoughts.
    Iago
                              I do beseech you,
Though I perchance am vicious in my guess—
As I confess it is my nature's plague
To spy into abuses, and oft my jealousy
Shapes faults that are not—that your wisdom then,
150 From one that so imperfectly conceits,

152 *scattering*: casual.
    observance: observation.
153 *quiet*: peace of mind.

157 *immediate*: most precious, nearest the
    heart.

160 *filches*: steals.

167 *jealousy*: suspicion of sexual infidelity.
168 *green-eyed monster*: green is
    traditionally the colour of jealousy.
168–9 *doth . . . feeds on*: torments its
    victim.
169 *That*: any.
    cuckold: man cheated (sexually) by
    his wife.
170 *certain of his fate*: sure that his wife
    has been false.
171 *damned*: damnèd.
    tells: counts.

175 *fineless*: infinite.
176 *ever*: always.

    Would take no notice, nor build yourself a trouble
    Out of his scattering and unsure observance.
    It were not for your quiet, nor your good,
    Nor for my manhood, honesty, and wisdom,
155 To let you know my thoughts.
    Othello
                             What dost thou mean?
    Iago
    Good name in man and woman, dear my lord,
    Is the immediate jewel of their souls.
    Who steals my purse, steals trash; 'tis something,
        nothing,
    'Twas mine, 'tis his, and has been slave to thousands:
160 But he that filches from me my good name
    Robs me of that which not enriches him
    And makes me poor indeed.
    Othello
    By heaven, I'll know thy thoughts.
    Iago
    You cannot, if my heart were in your hand,
165 Nor shall not, while 'tis in my custody.
    Othello
    Ha!
    Iago
    O beware, my lord, of jealousy:
    It is the green-eyed monster which doth mock
    The meat it feeds on. That cuckold lives in bliss
170 Who certain of his fate loves not his wronger;
    But O, what damned minutes tells he o'er
    Who dotes, yet doubts, suspects, yet fondly loves?
    Othello
    O misery!
    Iago
    Poor and content is rich, and rich enough;
175 But riches fineless is as poor as winter
    To him that ever fears he shall be poor.
    Good God, the souls of all my tribe defend
    From jealousy.
    Othello
                    Why, why is this?
    Think'st thou I'd make a life of jealousy,

'O beware, my lord, of jealousy: It is the green-eyed monster' (*3*, 3, 167–8). Richard McCabe as Iago and Ray Fearon as Othello, Royal Shakespeare Company, 1999.

180-1 *To follow . . . suspicions*: To
experience new doubts several times a
month, as the moon waxes and wanes.
181-2 *to be . . . resolv'd*: as soon as I have
any doubt, I will settle the question.
182 *a goat*: a creature reputedly lustful.
183 *turn . . . soul*: give my mind to
thinking.
184 *exsufflicate*: exaggerated, inflated; the
word is Othello's own coinage.
blown: fly-blown, rotten.
surmises: suspicions.
185 *Matching thy inference*: equal to your
interpretation.
'Tis not: It does not.
189 *weak merits*: lack of (physical)
attraction.
190 *revolt*: infidelity.

197 *franker*: more open.
bound: in duty bound to speak.
198 *Receive . . . me*: let me tell you.
199 *Look to*: take care of.
200 *secure*: over-confident.

202 *self-bounty*: innate generosity.
203 *country disposition*: national
(feminine) temperament.
204 *pranks*: sexual tricks.
205 *best conscience*: highest moral
standard.

208 *She . . . you*: Iago echoes the words of
Brabantio (*1, 3, 289-90*).

210 *go to*: there you are.
211 *Seeming*: pretence.
212 *seel*: blind (see *1, 3, 266* note).
oak: a hard, close-grained wood.

180 To follow still the changes of the moon
With fresh suspicions? No, to be once in doubt
Is once to be resolv'd. Exchange me for a goat
When I shall turn the business of my soul
To such exsufflicate and blown surmises
185 Matching thy inference. 'Tis not to make me jealous
To say my wife is fair, feeds well, loves company,
Is free of speech, sings, plays, and dances well:
Where virtue is, these are more virtuous.
Nor from mine own weak merits will I draw
190 The smallest fear or doubt of her revolt,
For she had eyes and chose me. No, Iago,
I'll see before I doubt; when I doubt, prove;
And on the proof, there is no more but this:
Away at once with love or jealousy!

Iago

195 I am glad of this; for now I shall have reason
To show the love and duty that I bear you
With franker spirit. Therefore, as I am bound
Receive it from me. I speak not yet of proof.
Look to your wife, observe her well with Cassio;
200 Wear your eyes thus: not jealous, nor secure.
I would not have your free and noble nature,
Out of self-bounty, be abus'd. Look to't.
I know our country disposition well:
In Venice they do let God see the pranks
205 They dare not show their husbands. Their best
conscience
Is not to leave't undone, but keep't unknown.

Othello

Dost thou say so?

Iago

She did deceive her father, marrying you;
And when she seem'd to shake and fear your looks
210 She lov'd them most.

Othello

                                            And so she did.

Iago

                                                                Why, go to then!
She that so young could give out such a seeming
To seel her father's eyes up close as oak

214-15 Please forgive me for loving you too much.

215 *bound*: indebted.

217 *Not a jot*: not at all.

219 *mov'd*: distressed.

220 *I am to pray you*: I must beg you.
strain: force.
221 *issues*: conclusions.
221-2 *nor to . . . suspicion*: extend beyond suspicion.

224 *fall . . . success*: have such a dreadful result.
225 *aim'd not at*: did not intend.

227 *honest*: chaste.

229 *erring from itself*: straying from its true self.

230 *bold*: blunt.
231 *affect*: like.
proposed: proposèd.
232 *clime*: country.

235 *disproportion*: impropriety.
236 *in position*: positively.
237 *Distinctly*: specifically.

He thought 'twas witchcraft—but I am much to
blame,
I humbly do beseech you of your pardon
215 For too much loving you.
  Othello
        I am bound to thee for ever.
  Iago
I see this hath a little dash'd your spirits.
  Othello
Not a jot, not a jot.
  Iago
      I'faith, I fear it has.
I hope you will consider what is spoke
Comes from my love. But I do see you're mov'd.
220 I am to pray you not to strain my speech
To grosser issues nor to larger reach
Than to suspicion.
  Othello
I will not.
  Iago
     Should you do so, my lord,
My speech should fall into such vile success
225 As my thoughts aim'd not at. Cassio's my worthy
friend—
My lord, I see you're mov'd.
  Othello
        No, not much mov'd.
I do not think but Desdemona's honest.
  Iago
Long live she so, and long live you to think so!
  Othello
And yet how nature erring from itself—
  Iago
230 Ay, there's the point: as, to be bold with you,
Not to affect many proposed matches
Of her own clime, complexion, and degree,
Whereto we see in all things nature tends—
Foh! one may smell, in such, a will most rank,
235 Foul disproportion, thoughts unnatural.
But pardon me: I do not in position
Distinctly speak of her; though I may fear

238 *recoiling*: returning.
239 *fall to match*: come to compare.
   her country forms: the appearances of
   her countrymen.
240 *happily*: perhaps.

245 *unfolds*: reveals.

247 *scan*: consider.
248 *place*: position (as lieutenant).
251 *means*: methods.
252 *strain . . . entertainment*: urges his
   reinstatement.
253 *importunity*: pleading.
255 *busy*: interfering.
257 *hold her free*: think her innocent.
258 *my government*: my self-control.
261 *qualities*: different kinds of men.
   with a learned spirit: learnèd; from
   experience.
262 *haggard*: a wild, untrained hawk.
263 *jesses*: the straps which secure the
   hawk's legs.

264 *whistle her off*: cast her off.
   let . . . wind: release her (as
   untrainable).
265 *prey at fortune*: take her own chances,
   look after herself.
   Haply: perhaps.
   for: because.
266 *soft . . . conversation*: easy social
   manners.
267 *chamberers*: gallants, ladies' men.
269 *abus'd*: deceived.
   relief: reaction.

Her will, recoiling to her better judgement,
May fall to match you with her country forms,
240 And happily repent.
     Othello
                         Farewell, farewell.
If more thou dost perceive, let me know more;
Set on thy wife to observe. Leave me, Iago.
     Iago
[*Going*] My lord, I take my leave.
     Othello
Why did I marry? This honest creature doubtless
245 Sees and knows more, much more, than he unfolds.
     Iago
[*Returning*] My lord, I would I might entreat your
     honour
To scan this thing no farther. Leave it to time.
Although 'tis fit that Cassio have his place—
For sure he fills it up with great ability—
250 Yet if you please to hold him off awhile,
You shall by that perceive him and his means.
Note if your lady strain his entertainment
With any strong or vehement importunity—
Much will be seen in that. In the mean time,
255 Let me be thought too busy in my fears—
As worthy cause I have to fear I am—
And hold her free, I do beseech your honour.
     Othello
Fear not my government.
     Iago
I once more take my leave.   [*Exit*
     Othello
260 This fellow's of exceeding honesty
And knows all qualities, with a learned spirit,
Of human dealings. If I do prove her haggard,
Though that her jesses were my dear heart-strings,
I'd whistle her off and let her down the wind
265 To prey at fortune. Haply for I am black,
And have not those soft parts of conversation
That chamberers have, or for I am declin'd
Into the vale of years—yet that's not much—
She's gone, I am abus'd, and my relief

270 Must be to loathe her. O curse of marriage,
That we can call these delicate creatures ours
And not their appetites! I had rather be a toad
And live upon the vapour of a dungeon
Than keep a corner in the thing I love
275 For others' uses. Yet 'tis the plague of great ones,
Prerogativ'd are they less than the base;
'Tis destiny unshunnable, like death:
Even then this forked plague is fated to us
When we do quicken. Look where she comes.

Enter Desdemona *and* Emilia

280 If she be false, O then heaven mocks itself;
I'll not believe it.
Desdemona
           How now, my dear Othello?
Your dinner and the generous islanders
By you invited, do attend your presence.
Othello
I am to blame.
Desdemona
           Why do you speak so faintly?
285 Are you not well?
Othello
I have a pain upon my forehead here.
Desdemona
Faith, that's with watching; 'twill away again.
Let me but bind it hard, within this hour
It will be well.
Othello
           Your napkin is too little.

He puts the handkerchief from him, and she drops it

290 Let it alone. Come, I'll go in with you.
Desdemona
I am very sorry that you are not well.
           [*Exeunt* Othello *and* Desdemona
Emilia
I am glad I have found this napkin:

272 *appetites*: desires.
    toad: traditionally a loathsome creature.
273 *vapour*: foul air; dungeons were often the sewers of a castle.
276 *Prerogativ'd . . . base*: with fewer opportunities than the humble (for privacy).
277 *destiny unshunnable*: inescapable fate.
278–9 *Even . . . quicken*: we are made cuckolds as soon as we are conceived.
278 *forked*: forkèd.

280 *mocks itself*: i.e. by the creation of something imperfect.

282 *generous*: noble.

286 *forehead*: i.e. where his cuckold's horns would grow.
287 *watching*: lack of sleep.

289 *napkin*: handkerchief.

This was her first remembrance from the Moor.
My wayward husband hath a hundred times
295 Woo'd me to steal it; but she so loves the token,
For he conjur'd her she should ever keep it,
That she reserves it evermore about her
To kiss and talk to. I'll have the work tane out
And give't Iago.
300 What he will do with it, heaven knows, not I:
I nothing but to please his fantasy.

   Enter Iago

  Iago
How now? What do you here alone?
  Emilia
Do not you chide; I have a thing for you.
  Iago
You have a thing for me? It is a common thing—
  Emilia
305 Ha!
  Iago
To have a foolish wife.
  Emilia
O, is that all? What will you give me now
For that same handkerchief?
  Iago
          What handkerchief?
  Emilia
What handkerchief!
310 Why, that the Moor first gave to Desdemona,
That which so often you did bid me steal.
  Iago
Hast stolen it from her?
  Emilia
No, faith; she let it drop by negligence,
And to th'advantage I being here took't up.
315 Look, here it is.
  Iago
      A good wench! Give it me.
  Emilia
What will you do with't, that you have been so earnest
To have me filch it?

---

294 *wayward*: unaccountable.
295 *Woo'd*: persuaded.
296 *conjur'd her*: made her swear.
297 *reserves*: keeps.
298 *work tane out*: embroidery copied.

301 *fantasy*: whim.

303 *a thing*: Emilia, flirting with Iago, uses the slang sense (= female sexual organ) of the word.
304 *common*: open to all.

314 *to th'advantage*: luckily.

317 *filch*: steal.

318 *import*: importance.

320 *lack it*: miss it.
Be . . . on't: say you know nothing
about it.

322 *lose*: drop.

324 *confirmations*: evidence.

325 *proofs of holy writ*: words from the
Bible.

327 *conceits*: imaginings.

328 *to distaste*: to be unpleasant.

329 *act*: action.

330 *mines of sulphur*: i.e. hell.

331 *poppy*: opium (derived from the
poppy).
mandragora: a narcotic deriving from
the mandrake plant.

332 *drowsy syrups*: soporific drugs.

333 *medicine*: drug.

334 *owed'st*: enjoyed.

336 *Avaunt*: get away.
rack: an instrument of torture that
stretched and twisted the limbs.

338 *but . . . little*: know only a part.

339 *sense*: awareness.

341 *free*: untroubled.

Iago
[*Snatching it*]   Why, what's that to you?
Emilia
If it be not for some purpose of import,
Give't me again. Poor lady, she'll run mad
320 When she shall lack it.
Iago
                              Be not acknown on't:
I have use for it. Go, leave me.   [*Exit* Emilia
I will in Cassio's lodging lose this napkin
And let him find it. Trifles light as air
Are to the jealous confirmations strong
325 As proofs of holy writ. This may do something.
The Moor already changes with my poison:
Dangerous conceits are in their natures poisons,
Which at the first are scarce found to distaste
But, with a little act upon the blood,
330 Burn like the mines of sulphur. I did say so.

Enter Othello

Look where he comes! Not poppy nor mandragora,
Nor all the drowsy syrups of the world,
Shall ever medicine thee to that sweet sleep
Which thou owed'st yesterday.
Othello
                              Ha, ha, false to me!
Iago
335 Why, how now, general! No more of that.
Othello
Avaunt, be gone! Thou hast set me on the rack.
I swear 'tis better to be much abus'd
Than but to know't a little.
Iago
                              How now, my lord!
Othello
What sense had I of her stolen hours of lust?
340 I saw't not, thought it not, it harm'd not me.
I slept the next night well, fed well, was free and merry;
I found not Cassio's kisses on her lips.

He that is robb'd, not wanting what is stolen,
Let him not know't and he's not robb'd at all.

Iago

345 I am sorry to hear this.

Othello

I had been happy if the general camp,
Pioners and all, had tasted her sweet body
So I had nothing known. O, now for ever
Farewell the tranquil mind! Farewell content!

350 Farewell the plumed troops, and the big wars
That makes ambition virtue—O farewell!
Farewell the neighing steed and the shrill trump,
The spirit-stirring drum, th'ear-piercing fife,
The royal banner, and all quality,

355 Pride, pomp, and circumstance of glorious war!
And, O you mortal engines, whose rude throats
Th'immortal Jove's dread clamours counterfeit,
Farewell! Othello's occupation's gone.

Iago

Is't possible, my lord?

Othello

360 Villain, be sure thou prove my love a whore;
Be sure of it. Give me the ocular proof,
Or by the worth of mine eternal soul,
Thou hadst been better have been born a dog
Than answer my wak'd wrath!

Iago

Is't come to this?

Othello

365 Make me to see't; or, at the least, so prove it
That the probation bear no hinge nor loop
To hang a doubt on—or woe upon thy life!

Iago

My noble lord—

Othello

If thou dost slander her and torture me,

370 Never pray more; abandon all remorse;
On horror's head horrors accumulate;
Do deeds to make heaven weep, all earth amaz'd:
For nothing canst thou to damnation add
Greater than that.

346 *the . . . camp*: the whole army.
347 *Pioners*: pioneers, considered the lowest form of soldier.
348 *So*: if only.
350 *plumed*: plumèd.
352 *trump*: trumpet.

354 *quality*: essential nature.
355 *circumstance*: ceremony.
356 *mortal engines*: deadly cannon.
     rude throats: loud voices.
357 *Jove . . . clamours*: i.e. thunder.
358 *occupation*: i.e. reason for living.
361 *Give . . . proof*: let me see with my own eyes.
364 *wak'd*: aroused.
366 *probation*: proof.

Iago

O grace! O heaven forgive me!

375 Are you a man? Have you a soul? Or sense?

God bu'y you; take mine office. O wretched fool,

That lov'st to make thine honesty a vice!

O monstrous world! Take note, take note, O world!

To be direct and honest is not safe.

380 I thank you for this profit, and from hence

I'll love no friend, sith love breeds such offence.

Othello

Nay, stay: thou shouldst be honest.

Iago

I should be wise; for honesty's a fool

And loses that it works for.

Othello

By the world,

385 I think my wife be honest, and think she is not;

I think that thou art just, and think thou art not.

I'll have some proof. Her name, that was as fresh

As Dian's visage, is now begrim'd and black

As mine own face. If there be cords or knives,

390 Poison or fire or suffocating streams,

I'll not endure it. Would I were satisfied!

Iago

I see, sir, you are eaten up with passion.

I do repent me that I put it to you.

You would be satisfied?

Othello

Would? Nay, I will.

Iago

395 And may. But how? How satisfied, my lord?

Would you, the supervisor, grossly gape on?

Behold her topp'd?

Othello

Death and damnation! O!

Iago

It were a tedious difficulty, I think,

To bring them to that prospect. Damn them then,

400 If ever mortal eyes do see them bolster

More than their own. What then? How then?

---

376 *God bu'y you*: God be with you.
take mine office: take away my appointment (as Othello's ensign or 'ancient').
fool: Iago addresses himself.
377 *vice*: fault.
379 *direct*: outspoken.
380 *profit*: lesson I have learned.
381 *sith*: since.
breeds such offence: causes such distress.

384 *that it works for*: the love which it tries to earn.

385 *honest*: chaste.
386 *just*: truthful.

388 *Dian*: Diana, virgin goddess of classical mythology.
begrim'd: dirtied.
389–91 *If . . . endure it*: Othello would resolve his uncertainties by suicide.
391 *Would I were satisfied*: I wish I were certain.

393 *put it*: suggested it.
394 *would*: want to be.

395 *How satisfied*: What would make you certain.
396 *the supervisor*: as an eye-witness.
grossly: crudely.
397 *topp'd*: with a man on top of her.

399 *prospect*: situation.
400 *bolster*: share a bed.
401 *More*: other.

What shall I say? Where's satisfaction?
It is impossible you should see this,
Were they as prime as goats, as hot as monkeys,
405 As salt as wolves in pride, and fools as gross
As Ignorance made drunk. But yet, I say,
If imputation and strong circumstances,
Which lead directly to the door of truth,
Will give you satisfaction, you might have't.
    Othello
410 Give me a living reason she's disloyal.
    Iago
I do not like the office;
But sith I am enter'd in this cause so far—
Prick'd to't by foolish honesty and love—
I will go on. I lay with Cassio lately,
415 And being troubled with a raging tooth
I could not sleep.
There are a kind of men so loose of soul
That in their sleeps will mutter their affairs.
One of this kind is Cassio.
420 In sleep I heard him say, 'Sweet Desdemona,
Let us be wary, let us hide our loves.'
And then, sir, he would gripe and wring my hand,
Cry, 'O sweet creature!' and then kiss me hard,
As if he pluck'd up kisses by the roots
425 That grew upon my lips; then laid his leg
Over my thigh, and sigh'd, and kiss'd, and then
Cried, 'Cursed fate that gave thee to the Moor.'
    Othello
O monstrous, monstrous!
    Iago
                           Nay, this was but his dream.
    Othello
But this denoted a foregone conclusion.
    Iago
430 'Tis a shrewd doubt, though it be but a dream;
And this may help to thicken other proofs
That do demonstrate thinly.
    Othello
                           I'll tear her all to pieces!

404 *prime*: lecherous.
    hot: lustful.
405 *salt . . . in pride*: keen as wolves on heat.
405–6 *fools . . . drunk*: such stupid fools as drunken ignorance.
407 *imputation . . . circumstances*: strong circumstantial evidence.
408 *to the door of truth*: in the direction of truth.
410 *living*: valid.

411 *office*: task.
412 *sith . . . far*: now that I have come so far with this business.
413 *Prick'd*: spurred.
414 *lay*: shared a bed.
415 *raging*: aching.

417 *loose*: indiscreet.

421 *wary*: careful.
422 *gripe*: grasp.

427 *Cursed*: cursèd.

429 *foregone conclusion*: previous consummation.

430 *shrewd doubt*: good guess.
    though . . . dream: although it was only a dream.
431 *thicken*: strengthen.
432 *do . . . thinly*: give weaker evidence.

Iago
Nay, yet be wise; yet we see nothing done,
She may be honest yet. Tell me but this:
435 Have you not sometimes seen a handkerchief
Spotted with strawberries in your wife's hand?
Othello
I gave her such a one; 'twas my first gift.
Iago
I know not that; but such a handkerchief—
I am sure it was your wife's—did I today
440 See Cassio wipe his beard with.
Othello
                                                    If it be that—
Iago
If it be that, or any that was hers,
It speaks against her with the other proofs.
Othello
O that the slave had forty thousand lives!
One is too poor, too weak, for my revenge.
445 Now do I see 'tis true. Look here, Iago,
All my fond love thus do I blow to heaven;
'Tis gone.
Arise, black vengeance, from thy hollow cell!
Yield up, O love, thy crown and hearted throne
450 To tyrannous hate! Swell, bosom, with thy fraught,
For 'tis of aspics' tongues.

He kneels

Iago
                                                    Yet be content.
Othello
O, blood, blood, blood!
Iago
Patience, I say; your mind perhaps may change.
Othello
Never, Iago. Like to the Pontic Sea,
455 Whose icy current and compulsive course
Ne'er feels retiring ebb but keeps due on
To the Propontic and the Hellespont,
Even so my bloody thoughts with violent pace

434 *yet*: still.

441 *any*: i.e. any handkerchief.
442 *speaks*: witnesses.

443 *the slave*: Othello refers to Cassio.

449 *hearted throne*: throne in my heart.
450 *fraught*: burden.
451 *aspics' tongues*: poisonous snakes (asps).
be content: calm down.

454 *Pontic sea*: the Black Sea.
455 *compulsive course*: irresistible force.
456 *Ne'er . . . ebb*: never ebbs back.
457 *the Propontic*: the Sea of Marmora.
the Hellespont: the Dardanelles.

460 *capable and wide*: suitably great.
461 *marble*: steadfast, unfeeling.

463 *engage*: pledge.

Shall ne'er look back, ne'er ebb to humble love,
460 Till that a capable and wide revenge
Swallow them up. Now by yond marble heaven,
In the due reverence of a sacred vow
I here engage my words.
 Iago
        Do not rise yet.

He kneels

464 *ever-burning lights*: i.e. the stars.
465 *elements . . . about*: the elements of fire, air, and water that enfold ('clip') the earth in the early cosmology.
467 *execution*: activity.
 wit: intellect.
469 *remorse*: compassion (because he is doing it for 'the wrong'd Othello').
470 *What . . . ever*: However murderous the task.
 greet: welcome.

Witness you ever-burning lights above,
465 You elements that clip us round about,
Witness that here Iago doth give up
The execution of his wit, hands, heart,
To wrong'd Othello's service. Let him command,
And to obey shall be in me remorse,
470 What bloody business ever.

They rise

Othello
       I greet thy love,

471 *vain*: empty.
 acceptance bounteous: generous reward.
472 *upon the instant*: immediately.
 put thee to't: put you to the test.

Not with vain thanks, but with acceptance bounteous;
And will upon the instant put thee to't.
Within these three days let me hear thee say
That Cassio's not alive.
 Iago
       My friend is dead;
475 'Tis done at your request. But let her live.
 Othello
Damn her, lewd minx! O, damn her, damn her!

477 *apart*: aside.
478 *furnish me*: equip myself.
479 *Now . . . lieutenant*: Iago has achieved the military position he desired.

Come, go with me apart. I will withdraw
To furnish me with some swift means of death
For the fair devil. Now art thou my lieutenant.
 Iago
480 I am your own for ever.   [*Exeunt*

Act 3 Scene 4

Desdemona persists in the recommendation of Cassio, but Othello is obsessed with the handkerchief; Iago and Cassio pass along the street, and Cassio is met by his mistress Bianca—to whom he gives Othello's handkerchief.

1 *lies*: a) lodges; b) speaks falsely.

7 *lie*: deceive.

10–11 *lie . . . throat*: tell a deliberate lie.

12 *edified*: instructed (as by the question-and-answer teaching of the Christian catechism).

15 *moved*: persuaded.

17 *compass*: scope, range.

SCENE 4

The street outside Othello's lodging: enter
Desdemona, Emilia, *and* Clown

Desdemona
Do you know, sirrah, where Lieutenant Cassio lies?
Clown
I dare not say he lies anywhere.
Desdemona
Why, man?
Clown
He's a soldier, and for one to say a soldier lies is
5 stabbing.
Desdemona
Go to. Where lodges he?
Clown
To tell you where he lodges is to tell you where I lie.
Desdemona
Can anything be made of this?
Clown
I know not where he lodges, and for me to devise a
10 lodging, and say he lies here, or he lies there, were to lie
in mine own throat.
Desdemona
Can you enquire him out, and be edified by report?
Clown
I will catechize the world for him: that is, make
questions, and by them answer.
Desdemona
15 Seek him; bid him come hither; tell him I have moved
my lord on his behalf and hope all will be well.
Clown
To do this is within the compass of man's wit, and
therefore I will attempt the doing of it. [*Exit*
Desdemona
Where should I lose that handkerchief, Emilia?
Emilia
20 I know not, madam.

22 *crusadoes*: Portuguese gold coins
   stamped with a cross.
   but: except.

27 *humours*: bodily fluids influencing
   temperament (here black bile, causing
   melancholy).

32 *moist*: A moist palm was believed to
   indicate youthfulness and sexual
   ardour.

34 *argues*: is proof of.
   liberal: a) generous; b) licentious.

36 *sequester*: restraint (a legal term).
37 *castigation*: corrective discipline.

40 *frank*: a) honest; b) revealing.

Desdemona
Believe me, I had rather lose my purse
Full of crusadoes; and but my noble Moor
Is true of mind and made of no such baseness
As jealous creatures are, it were enough
25 To put him to ill thinking.
  Emilia
         Is he not jealous?
Desdemona
Who, he? I think the sun where he was born
Drew all such humours from him.

Enter Othello

  Emilia
        Look where he comes.
Desdemona
I will not leave him now; let Cassio
Be call'd to him.—How is't with you, my lord?
  Othello
30 Well, my good lady. [*Aside*] O hardness to dissemble!
How do you, Desdemona?
  Desdemona
        Well, my good lord.
  Othello
Give me your hand. This hand is moist, my lady.
  Desdemona
It yet hath felt no age, nor known no sorrow.
  Othello
This argues fruitfulness and liberal heart.
35 Hot, hot, and moist. This hand of yours requires
A sequester from liberty, fasting and prayer,
Much castigation, exercise devout;
For here's a young and sweating devil here
That commonly rebels. 'Tis a good hand,
40 A frank one.
  Desdemona
     You may indeed say so,
For 'twas that hand that gave away my heart.

42–3 *The hearts . . . hearts*: Othello
seems to refer to the modern orders of
chivalry, suggesting a contrast
between the sincere 'hearts' and the
token 'hands'.

44 *speak of*: understand.

45 *chuck*: a term of endearment.

47 *salt . . . rheum*: a) miserable running
cold; b) lustful humour.

52 *Egyptian*: These were believed to be
the ancestors of modern gypsies.

53 *charmer*: enchantress.

55 *amiable*: desirable, beloved.

58 *loathed*: loathèd.
spirits: desires.

60 *my fate . . . wive*: it should be my
fortune to marry.

63 *perdition*: disaster.

64 *match*: equal.

Othello
A liberal hand! The hearts of old gave hands;
But our new heraldry is hands, not hearts.
   Desdemona
I cannot speak of this. Come now, your promise.
   Othello
45 What promise, chuck?
   Desdemona
I have sent to bid Cassio come speak with you.
   Othello
I have a salt and sorry rheum offends me;
Lend me thy handkerchief.
   Desdemona
                Here, my lord.
   Othello
That which I gave you.
   Desdemona
              I have it not about me.
   Othello
50 Not?
   Desdemona
No, faith, my lord.
   Othello
           That's a fault. That handkerchief
Did an Egyptian to my mother give:
She was a charmer and could almost read
The thoughts of people. She told her, while she kept it,
55 'Twould make her amiable and subdue my father
Entirely to her love; but if she lost it
Or made a gift of it, my father's eye
Should hold her loathed and his spirits should hunt
After new fancies. She dying gave it me,
60 And bid me when my fate would have me wive,
To give it her. I did so, and take heed on't:
Make it a darling, like your precious eye.
To lose't or give't away were such perdition
As nothing else could match.
   Desdemona
                 Is't possible?

65 *web*: weaving.
66 *sibyl*: prophetess.
66–7 *that had . . . compasses*: i.e. she was two hundred years old.
68 *prophetic fury*: frenzy of inspiration.
69 *hallow'd*: sacred.
70 *mummy*: mummia—a preparation made from mummified dead bodies.
71 *Conserv'd of*: prepared as a drug from.

72 *look to't well*: take good care of it.

73 *would*: I wish.

75 *startingly and rash*: abruptly and violently.

76 *out o'th'way*: missing.

78 *Say you*: What do you say?

79 *and if*: if perhaps.

83 *to put . . . suit*: make me forget what I wanted.

85 *misgives*: fears the worst.

87 *sufficient*: competent.

Othello

65   'Tis true. There's magic in the web of it:
     A sibyl, that had number'd in the world
     The sun to course two hundred compasses,
     In her prophetic fury sew'd the work;
     The worms were hallow'd that did breed the silk,
70   And it was dyed in mummy, which the skilful
     Conserv'd of maidens' hearts.

Desdemona

                               I'faith, is't true?

Othello

     Most veritable; therefore look to't well.

Desdemona

     Then would to God that I had never seen't!

Othello

     Ha? Wherefore?

Desdemona

75   Why do you speak so startingly and rash?

Othello

     Is't lost? Is't gone? Speak; is't out of th'way?

Desdemona

     Heaven bless us!

Othello

     Say you?

Desdemona

     It is not lost, but what and if it were?

Othello

80   How?

Desdemona

     I say it is not lost.

Othello

                               Fetch't, let me see't.

Desdemona

     Why so I can, sir; but I will not now.
     This is a trick to put me from my suit.
     Pray you let Cassio be receiv'd again.

Othello

85   Fetch me the handkerchief. My mind misgives.

Desdemona

     Come, come;
     You'll never meet a more sufficient man.

'Fetch me the handkerchief. My mind misgives' (3, 4, 85). Willard White as Othello, Royal Shakespeare Company, 1989.

Othello
The handkerchief!
Desdemona
                            I pray, talk me of Cassio.
Othello
The handkerchief!
Desdemona
                            A man that all his time

90 *founded*: based.

90 Hath founded his good fortunes on your love,
Shared dangers with you—
Othello
The handkerchief!
Desdemona
                            I'faith, you are to blame.
Othello
Zounds!   [*Exit*
Emilia
Is not this man jealous?
Desdemona
                            I ne'er saw this before.

95 *wonder*: magic.

95 Sure there's some wonder in this handkerchief;
I am most unhappy in the loss of it.
Emilia
'Tis not a year or two shows us a man.

97 *'Tis . . . man*: It doesn't take very long
for us to know what men are like.
98 *but stomachs*: only appetites.
99 *hungerly*: hungrily.

They are all but stomachs, and we all but food;
They eat us hungerly, and when they are full,
100 They belch us.

Enter Iago *and* Cassio

                            Look you, Cassio and my husband.
Iago
There is no other way: 'tis she must do't.

102 *the happiness*: good luck.

And lo, the happiness! Go, and importune her.
Desdemona
How now, good Cassio! What's the news with you?
Cassio
Madam, my former suit. I do beseech you

105 *virtuous*: efficacious.
106 *Exist*: be myself.
107 *office*: loyalty.

105 That, by your virtuous means, I may again
Exist and be a member of his love,
Whom I, with all the office of my heart,

108 *I would not be delay'd*: I don't want to
     waste time.
109 *mortal*: deadly.
110 *nor . . . nor*: neither . . . nor.
111 *purpos'd merit*: what I intend to
     deserve.
     in futurity: in times to come.
112 *ransom*: buy my way back.
113 *But*: merely.
     benefit: i.e. because he must know
     the worst.
114 Then I shall have to be satisfied with
     that.
115 *shut myself up*: confine.
     some other course: a different career.
116 *To fortune's alms*: to accept whatever
     fortune can spare.
117 *advocation*: advocacy.
     in tune: suitable.
119 *favour*: appearance.
     humour: temper.
120 *So . . . sanctified*: may all the angels
     witness.
121 *As*: that.
     all my best: to the best of my ability.
122 *within the blank*: at the centre of the
     target (in archery).
123 *free speech*: outspokenness.

132 *of moment*: very important.
133 *There's . . . indeed*: it's serious then.

134 *of state*: concerning state affairs.
135 *unhatch'd practice*: undisclosed plot.
136 *demonstrable*: obvious.
137 *puddled*: disturbed.
138 *wrangle with*: quarrel over.
139 *object*: main concern.
140–2 *let . . . pain*: if our finger aches, it
     makes the whole body hurt.

Entirely honour. I would not be delay'd.
If my offence be of such mortal kind

110 That nor my service past nor present sorrows,
Nor purpos'd merit in futurity,
Can ransom me into his love again,
But to know so must be my benefit:
So shall I clothe me in a forced content,

115 And shut myself up in some other course
To fortune's alms.
       Desdemona
                    Alas, thrice-gentle Cassio,
My advocation is not now in tune:
My lord is not my lord; nor should I know him,
Were he in favour as in humour alter'd.

120 So help me every spirit sanctified,
As I have spoken for you all my best,
And stood within the blank of his displeasure
For my free speech! You must awhile be patient.
What I can do, I will; and more I will

125 Than for myself I dare. Let that suffice you.
       Iago
Is my lord angry?
       Emilia
                    He went hence but now
And certainly in strange unquietness.
       Iago
Can he be angry? I have seen the cannon
When it hath blown his ranks into the air,

130 And like the devil from his very arm
Puff'd his own brother—and is he angry?
Something of moment then. I will go meet him.
There's matter in't indeed if he be angry.
       Desdemona
I prithee do so.   [*Exit* Iago
                    Something sure of state,

135 Either from Venice, or some unhatch'd practice
Made demonstrable here in Cyprus to him,
Hath puddled his clear spirit; and in such cases
Men's natures wrangle with inferior things,
Though great ones are their object. 'Tis even so;

140 For let our finger ache, and it endues

Our other healthful members even to a sense
Of pain. Nay, we must think men are not gods,
Nor of them look for such observancy
As fits the bridal. Beshrew me much, Emilia,
145 I was—unhandsome warrior as I am—
Arraigning his unkindness with my soul;
But now I find I had suborn'd the witness
And he's indicted falsely.
      Emilia
Pray heaven it be state matters, as you think,
150 And no conception nor no jealous toy
Concerning you.
            Desdemona
Alas the day, I never gave him cause.
      Emilia
But jealous souls will not be answer'd so.
They are not ever jealous for the cause,
155 But jealous for they're jealous. 'Tis a monster
Begot upon itself, born on itself.
      Desdemona
Heaven keep that monster from Othello's mind.
      Emilia
Lady, amen!
      Desdemona
I will go seek him. Cassio, walk here about.
160 If I do find him fit, I'll move your suit
And seek to effect it to my uttermost.
      Cassio
I humbly thank your ladyship.
                  [*Exeunt* Desdemona *and* Emilia

Enter Bianca

      Bianca
'Save you, friend Cassio.
      Cassio
                  What make you from home?
How is it with you, my most fair Bianca?
165 I'faith, sweet love, I was coming to your house.

---

143 *of them*: from them.
   observancy: attentiveness.
144 *the bridal*: the wedding-night.
   Beshrew me: a mild oath.
145 *unhandsome warrior*: unskilled soldier;
   Desdemona remembers how Othello
   called her his 'fair warrior' when he
   greeted her in Cyprus (*2, 1, 175*).
146 *Arraigning*: accusing.
   unkindness: unnatural behaviour.
147 *suborn'd the witness*: caused the
   witness [i.e. herself] to give false
   evidence.
148 *indicted*: accused.
150 *conception*: fantasy.
   toy: fancy.

154 *ever*: always.
   for the cause: for some reason.
155 *for*: because.
   'Tis: Emilia echoes her husband's
   description of the monster which is
   the personification of jealousy.

163 *'Save you*: may God save you.
   What . . . home?: What are you doing
   away from home?

164 *How . . . you?*: How are you?

167 *a week*: It would seem that a week has elapsed between this scene and the previous one.
168 *lovers' absent hours*: the hours when lovers are away from each other.
169 *dial*: clock.

171 *leaden . . . press'd*: tortured by heavy thoughts (as a traitor was pressed to death with heavy weights).
172 *continuate*: uninterrupted.
173 *Strike . . . score*: pay off this debt.
174 *Take . . . out*: copy out this embroidery.
whence came this?: where did you get this?
175 *token*: i.e. love-token.
friend: i.e. mistress.

188 *no addition*: no honourable title.
189 *woman'd*: with a woman.

Bianca
And I was going to your lodging, Cassio.
What! Keep a week away? Seven days and nights?
Eight score eight hours? And lovers' absent hours
More tedious than the dial eight score times!
170 O weary reckoning!
Cassio
                Pardon me, Bianca.
I have this while with leaden thoughts been press'd
But I shall in a more continuate time
Strike off this score of absence. Sweet Bianca,
Take me this work out.
Bianca
             O Cassio, whence came this?
175 This is some token from a newer friend.
To the felt absence now I feel a cause.
Is't come to this? Well, well.
Cassio
                Go to, woman!
Throw your vile guesses in the devil's teeth
From whence you have them. You are jealous now
180 That this is from some mistress, some remembrance.
No, by my faith, Bianca.
Bianca
             Why, whose is it?
Cassio
I know not neither; I found it in my chamber.
I like the work well. Ere it be demanded—
As like enough it will—I'd have it copied.
185 Take it and do't, and leave me for this time.
Bianca
Leave you? Wherefore?
Cassio
I do attend here on the general;
And think it no addition, nor my wish,
To have him see me woman'd.
Bianca
            Why, I pray you?
Cassio
190 Not that I love you not.

Bianca

But that you do not love me.
I pray you, bring me on the way a little,
And say if I shall see you soon at night.

Cassio

'Tis but a little way that I can bring you,
For I attend here; but I'll see you soon.

Bianca

195 'Tis very good; I must be circumstanc'd.   [*Exeunt*

191 *bring*: accompany.

195 *circumstanc'd*: accept the situation.

ACT 4

Act 4 Scene 1
Iago continues to prompt Othello's jealousy and Othello overhears Iago teasing Cassio about some woman—whom Othello assumes to be Desdemona. Lodovico is outraged when he sees Othello strike Desdemona.

SCENE 1

A street: enter Othello *and* Iago

Iago
Will you think so?
   Othello
Think so, Iago?
   Iago
          What,
To kiss in private?
   Othello
An unauthoriz'd kiss!
   Iago
Or to be naked with her friend in bed
An hour or more, not meaning any harm?
   Othello
5 Naked in bed, Iago, and not mean harm?
It is hypocrisy against the devil.
They that mean virtuously and yet do so,
The devil their virtue tempts, and they tempt heaven.
   Iago
So they do nothing, 'tis a venial slip;
10 But if I give my wife a handkerchief—
   Othello
What then?
   Iago
Why, then 'tis hers, my lord; and being hers,
She may, I think, bestow't on any man.
   Othello
She is protectress of her honour too.
15 May she give that?
   Iago
Her honour is an essence that's not seen:
They have it very oft that have it not.
But for the handkerchief—

3 *friend*: lover.

6 *hypocrisy . . . devil*: i.e. they would be cheating the devil if they are virtuous and pretend to be sinful—as pretence of good to conceal evil is hypocrisy against God.
8 *tempt heaven*: i.e. tempt God to curse them.
9 *So*: if, so long as.
  venial slip: trivial mistake (not a deadly sin).

16 *essence*: spiritual entity.
17 *have . . . not*: i.e. are credited with honour although they have lost it.

Othello
By heaven, I would most gladly have forgot it.
20 Thou said'st—O it comes o'er my memory,
As doth the raven o'er the infected house,
Boding to all!—he had my handkerchief.
  Iago
Ay, what of that?
  Othello
                    That's not so good now.
  Iago
                                        What
If I had said I had seen him do you wrong?
25 Or heard him say—as knaves be such abroad,
Who having by their own importunate suit
Or voluntary dotage of some mistress
Convinced or supplied them, cannot choose
But they must blab—
  Othello
                        Hath he said anything?
  Iago
30 He hath, my lord; but be you well assur'd
No more than he'll unswear.
  Othello
                              What hath he said?
  Iago
Faith, that he did—I know not what he did.
  Othello
What, what?
  Iago
Lie—
  Othello
    With her?
  Iago
              With her, on her, what you will.
  Othello
35 Lie with her? Lie on her? We say lie on her when they
belie her. Lie with her! Zounds, that's fulsome!
Handkerchief—confessions—handkerchief! To confess
and be hanged for his labour. First to be hanged and
then to confess. I tremble at it. Nature would not invest
40 herself in such shadowing passion without some

21 *raven*: traditionally a bird of ill omen (thought to perch above the houses of those sick with the plague).
22 *Boding all*: prophesying doom to all.

25 *as . . . abroad*: as there are such villains about.
26 *importunate*: demanding.
27 *voluntary dotage*: willing infatuation.
28 *Convinced*: convincèd; overcome. *supplied*: sexually satisfied.

36 *belie*: slander. *fulsome*: disgusting.
37–8 *confess . . . labour*: proverbial.
38–9 *First . . . confess*: Othello seems to conceive of Cassio's not being given the proper 'shriving time' before he is executed.
39–41 *Nature . . . instruction*: my natural faculties would not overwhelm themselves in such vague passion without reason.

42 *Noses . . . lips*: Othello may be
thinking that their noses and lips may
have touched in kissing, and their ears
have been close together for
whispering.

47 *reproach*: shame.

53 *lethargy*: coma, unconsciousness.

58 *on great occasion*: about a serious
matter.

60 *Dost . . . me*: Othello thinks Iago
refers to the cuckold's horns.

61 *Would*: I wish.
your fortune: i.e. in having a faithless
wife.
62 *horned man*: hornèd; i.e. a cuckold.

instruction. It is not words that shakes me thus. Pish!
Noses, ears, and lips. Is't possible?—Confess?
Handkerchief? O devil!

He falls in a trance

Iago
Work on,
45 My medicine, work! Thus credulous fools are caught;
And many worthy and chaste dames even thus,
All guiltless, meet reproach. What ho, my lord!
My lord, I say! Othello!

Enter Cassio

How now, Cassio!
Cassio
What's the matter?
Iago
50 My lord is fallen into an epilepsy.
This is his second fit; he had one yesterday.
Cassio
Rub him about the temples.
Iago
No, forbear.
The lethargy must have his quiet course.
If not, he foams at mouth and by and by
55 Breaks out to savage madness. Look, he stirs.
Do you withdraw yourself a little while;
He will recover straight. When he is gone,
I would on great occasion speak with you.
[*Exit* Cassio
How is it, general? Have you not hurt your head?
Othello
60 Dost thou mock me?
Iago
I mock you? No, by heaven!
Would you would bear your fortune like a man!
Othello
A horned man's a monster and a beast.

64 *civil*: civilized.

66 *yok'd*: a) married; b) burdened.
67 *draw*: a) pull (the plough); b) share.
68 *unproper*: not solely their own (because shared by wife's lovers).
69 *peculiar*: their own.
   better: i.e. because he knows he is cheated.
70 *arch-mock*: supreme mockery.
71 *lip*: kiss.
   wanton: faithless woman.
   secure: free from suspicion.
73 *what I am*: i.e. a cuckold.

75 *in . . . list*: within the bounds of self-control ('list' = barrier).
76 *o'erwhelmed*: o'erwhelmèd.

78 *shifted him away*: got rid of him by stratagem.
79 *laid good scuse*: made a good excuse of.
   ecstasy: fit, trance.
80 *anon*: immediately.
81 *encave*: conceal.
82 *fleers*: mocks.
   notable: obvious.

86 *cope*: encounter, copulate with.
87 *gesture*: behaviour.
88 *all . . . spleen*: consumed with passion (thought to reside in the spleen).

90 *cunning*: crafty.

92 *keep time*: be controlled (a musical term).

Iago
There's many a beast then in a populous city,
And many a civil monster.
   Othello
65 Did he confess it?
   Iago
                Good sir, be a man:
Think every bearded fellow that's but yok'd
May draw with you. There's millions now alive
That nightly lie in those unproper beds
Which they dare swear peculiar. Your case is better.
70 O, 'tis the spite of hell, the fiend's arch-mock,
To lip a wanton in a secure couch
And to suppose her chaste! No, let me know;
And knowing what I am, I know what she shall be.
   Othello
O, thou art wise; 'tis certain.
   Iago
                  Stand you awhile apart,
75 Confine yourself but in a patient list.
Whilst you were here, o'erwhelmed with your grief—
A passion most unsuiting such a man—
Cassio came hither. I shifted him away
And laid good scuse upon your ecstasy;
80 Bade him anon return and here speak with me,
The which he promis'd. Do but encave yourself,
And mark the fleers, the gibes, and notable scorns
That dwell in every region of his face;
For I will make him tell the tale anew,
85 Where, how, how oft, how long ago, and when
He hath and is again to cope your wife.
I say but mark his gesture. Marry, patience,
Or I shall say you're all in all in spleen
And nothing of a man.
   Othello
                  Dost thou hear, Iago?
90 I will be found most cunning in my patience,
But—dost thou hear—most bloody.
   Iago
                  That's not amiss.
But yet keep time in all. Will you withdraw?

Othello *withdraws*

93 *of*: about; Iago explains his tactics to the audience.
94 *housewife*: hussy (pronounced 'huswif').
desires: sexual desires.

Now will I question Cassio of Bianca,
A housewife that by selling her desires
95 Buys herself bread and clothes. It is a creature
That dotes on Cassio; as 'tis the strumpet's plague
To beguile many and be beguil'd by one.
He, when he hears of her, cannot refrain
From the excess of laughter. Here he comes.

Enter Cassio

101 *unbookish*: ignorant (compared with Iago's worldly wisdom).
construe: interpret.
102 *light*: cheerful.

104 *addition*: title.
105 *Whose want*: the lack of which.

100 As he shall smile, Othello shall go mad;
And his unbookish jealousy must construe
Poor Cassio's smiles, gestures, and light behaviours
Quite in the wrong. How do you now, lieutenant?
Cassio
The worser that you give me the addition
105 Whose want even kills me.
Iago
Ply Desdemona well and you are sure on't.
Now if this suit lay in Bianca's power,
How quickly should you speed!

108 *speed*: prosper.
caitiff: wretch (affectionate).

Cassio
                                        Alas, poor caitiff!
Othello
[*Aside*] Look how he laughs already!
Iago
110 I never knew a woman love man so.
Cassio
Alas, poor rogue! I think, i'faith, she loves me.
Othello

112 *faintly*: lightly.

[*Aside*] Now he denies it faintly, and laughs it out.
Iago
Do you hear, Cassio?
Othello
[*Aside*]   Now he importunes him

114 *said*: done.

To tell it o'er. Go to, well said, well said!
Iago

115 *gives it out*: tells people.

115 She gives it out that you shall marry her.
Do you intend it?

118 *Roman*: conqueror.

119 *customer*: whore.
119–20 *bear . . . wit*: think better of my judgement.
120 *unwholesome*: unhealthy, feeble.

122 *So, so, so*: The call of a huntsman encouraging his hounds.

123 *cry*: rumour (and the call of hounds picking up the scent).

125 *very*: true.

126 *scored*: wounded, marked.

128 *out . . . flattery*: by her own flattering self-love.

131 *even now*: just now.

133 *bauble*: plaything.
134 *falls . . . neck*: throws her arms round my neck.

136 *imports*: suggests.

137 *hales*: tugs.

139 *plucked*: drew.

142 *leave her company*: stop seeing her.

Cassio
Ha, ha, ha!
Othello
[*Aside*] Do you triumph, Roman? Do you triumph?
Cassio
I marry her? What! A customer! I prithee, bear some
120 charity to my wit. Do not think it so unwholesome. Ha, ha, ha!
Othello
[*Aside*] So, so, so, so: they laugh that wins.
Iago
Faith, the cry goes that you shall marry her.
Cassio
Prithee, say true.
Iago
125 I am a very villain else.
Othello
[*Aside*] Have you scored me? Well.
Cassio
This is the monkey's own giving out. She is persuaded I
will marry her out of her own love and flattery, not out
of my promise.
Othello
130 [*Aside*] Iago beckons me. Now he begins the story.
Cassio
She was here even now. She haunts me in every place. I
was the other day talking on the sea-bank with certain
Venetians, and thither comes this bauble and, by this
hand, falls me thus about my neck.
Othello
135 [*Aside*] Crying 'O dear Cassio!' as it were. His gesture
imports it.
Cassio
So hangs and lolls and weeps upon me, so hales and
pulls me. Ha, ha, ha!
Othello
[*Aside*] Now he tells how she plucked him to my
140 chamber. O, I see that nose of yours, but not that dog I
shall throw it to!
Cassio
Well, I must leave her company.

143 *Before me*: An exclamation of surprise
(= Upon my soul!).

144 *such another*: no other than.
fitchew: polecat, a creature noted for
its smell when sexually aroused.
perfumed: prostitutes were often
highly scented.

146 *dam*: mother (a proverbial expression).

148 *take out*: copy.

149 *piece of work*: story.

152 *hobby-horse*: whore.

155 *should*: must.

157 *when . . . for*: when you are next
expected (i.e. never).

159 *rail*: shout.
else: otherwise.

162 *very fain*: very much like to.

166 *Go to*: you bet.

Iago
Before me, look where she comes!
    Cassio
'Tis such another fitchew! Marry, a perfumed one.

Enter Bianca

145 What do you mean by this haunting of me?
    Bianca
Let the devil and his dam haunt you! What did you
mean by that same handkerchief you gave me even
now? I was a fine fool to take it. I must take out the
work? A likely piece of work that you should find it in
150 your chamber and not know who left it there! This is
some minx's token, and I must take out the work?
There, give it your hobby-horse, wheresoever you had
it. I'll take out no work on't.
    Cassio
How now, my sweet Bianca! How now, how now!
    Othello
155 [*Aside*] By heaven, that should be my handkerchief!
    Bianca
If you'll come to supper tonight, you may. If you will
not, come when you are next prepared for.   [*Exit*
    Iago
After her, after her!
    Cassio
Faith, I must. She'll rail in the streets else.
    Iago
160 Will you sup there?
    Cassio
Faith, I intend so.
    Iago
Well, I may chance to see you; for I would very fain
speak with you.
    Cassio
Prithee, come; will you?
    Iago
165 Go to; say no more.   [*Exit* Cassio
    Othello
[*Coming forward*] How shall I murder him, Iago?

Iago

Did you perceive how he laughed at his vice?

Othello

O, Iago!

Iago

And did you see the handkerchief?

Othello

170 Was that mine?

Iago

171 *by this hand*: The common oath (= I swear it) is also the literal truth.

Yours, by this hand. And to see how he prizes the foolish woman your wife: she gave it to him, and he hath given it his whore.

Othello

174 *a-killing*: being killed.

I would have him nine years a-killing. A fine woman, a
175 fair woman, a sweet woman!

Iago

Nay, you must forget that.

Othello

Ay, let her rot and perish, and be damned tonight, for she shall not live. No, my heart is turned to stone: I strike it and it hurts my hand. O, the world hath not a
180 sweeter creature! She might lie by an emperor's side and command him tasks.

Iago

182 *your way*: your proper course of action.

Nay, that's not your way.

Othello

Hang her, I do but say what she is: so delicate with her needle, an admirable musician—O, she will sing the
185 savageness out of a bear—of so high and plenteous wit

186 *invention*: imagination.

and invention—

Iago

She's the worse for all this.

Othello

188-9 *gentle a condition*: a) well-bred; b) mild a temperament.

O, a thousand, thousand times—and then of so gentle a condition!

Iago

190 *too gentle*: i.e. too yielding.

190 Ay, too gentle.

Othello

Nay, that's certain; but yet the pity of it, Iago! O, Iago, the pity of it, Iago!

'Did you perceive how he laughed at his vice?' (4, 1, 167). Ian McKellen as Iago and Willard White as Othello, Royal Shakespeare Company, 1989.

193 *fond over*: foolish about.
   patent: licence.
194 *if . . . nobody*: if it doesn't hurt you, it
   won't affect anyone else.
195 *messes*: little bits of meat.

200 *expostulate*: argue.
201 *unprovide*: weaken.

205 *be his undertaker*: deal with him.

Iago
If you are so fond over her iniquity, give her patent to
offend; for if it touch not you, it comes near nobody.
Othello
195 I will chop her into messes. Cuckold me!
Iago
O, 'tis foul in her.
Othello
With mine officer!
Iago
That's fouler.
Othello
Get me some poison, Iago, this night. I'll not
200 expostulate with her, lest her body and beauty
unprovide my mind again—this night, Iago.
Iago
Do it not with poison; strangle her in her bed, even the
bed she hath contaminated.
Othello
Good, good! The justice of it pleases; very good!
Iago
205 And for Cassio, let me be his undertaker. You shall hear
more by midnight.
Othello
Excellent good!

A trumpet sounds within

What trumpet is that same?
Iago
I warrant something from Venice.

Enter Lodovico, Desdemona, *and* Attendants

210 'Tis Lodovico. This comes from the duke. See, your
wife's with him.
Lodovico
God save you, worthy general!
Othello
                                    With all my heart, sir.

Lodovico
The duke and senators of Venice greet you.

He gives Othello *a letter*

Othello
I kiss the instrument of their pleasures.

He opens the letter and reads

Desdemona
215 And what's the news, good cousin Lodovico?
    Iago
I am very glad to see you, signior;
Welcome to Cyprus.
    Lodovico
I thank you. How does Lieutenant Cassio?
    Iago
Lives, sir.
    Desdemona
220 Cousin, there's fallen between him and my lord
An unkind breach; but you shall make all well.
    Othello
Are you sure of that?
    Desdemona
My lord?
    Othello
'This fail you not to do, as you will—'
    Lodovico
225 He did not call; he's busy in the paper.
Is there division 'twixt my lord and Cassio?
    Desdemona
A most unhappy one; I would do much
T'atone them, for the love I bear to Cassio.
    Othello
Fire and brimstone!
    Desdemona
230 My lord?
    Othello
Are you wise?
    Desdemona
What, is he angry?

---

214 *I . . . pleasures*: Othello demonstrates his respect for the state of Venice.

221 *unkind breach*: unnatural separation.

225 *in the paper*: reading the letter.
226 *division*: difference of opinion.

228 *atone*: bring them together.

Lodovico
                    Maybe the letter mov'd him;
For as I think they do command him home,
Deputing Cassio in his government.
    Desdemona
235 By my troth, I am glad on't.
    Othello
                            Indeed!
    Desdemona
                                My lord?
    Othello
I am glad to see you mad.
    Desdemona
                        Why, sweet Othello?
    Othello
Devil!

He strikes her

    Desdemona
I have not deserv'd this.
    Lodovico
My lord, this would not be believ'd in Venice,
240 Though I should swear I saw't. 'Tis very much.
Make her amends; she weeps.
    Othello
                            O devil, devil!
If that the earth could teem with woman's tears,
Each drop she falls would prove a crocodile.
Out of my sight!
    Desdemona
                    I will not stay to offend you.
    Lodovico
245 Truly, an obedient lady.
I do beseech your lordship, call her back.
    Othello
Mistress!
    Desdemona
My lord?
    Othello
What would you with her, sir?

240 *very much*: outrageous.

242 *teem*: be impregnated.

243 *falls*: lets fall.
prove: a) turn into; b) be like those of a crocodile (notorious for shedding false tears to deceive its prey).

247 *Mistress!*: Othello calls to Desdemona as though she were a prostitute in a brothel.

Lodovico

Who? I, my lord?

Othello

250 Ay, you did wish that I would make her turn.
Sir, she can turn, and turn, and yet go on,
And turn again. And she can weep, sir, weep.
And she's obedient; as you say, obedient,
Very obedient—proceed you in your tears—
255 Concerning this, sir,—O, well-painted passion!—
I am commanded home—get you away!
I'll send for you anon.—Sir, I obey the mandate,
And will return to Venice.—Hence, avaunt!

[*Exit* Desdemona

Cassio shall have my place. And, sir, tonight
260 I do entreat that we may sup together.
You are welcome, sir, to Cyprus. Goats and monkeys!

[*Exit*

Lodovico

Is this the noble Moor whom our full senate
Call all-in-all sufficient? Is this the nature
Whom passion could not shake? Whose solid virtue
265 The shot of accident nor dart of chance
Could neither graze nor pierce?

Iago

He is much chang'd.

Lodovico

Are his wits safe? Is he not light of brain?

Iago

He's that he is; I may not breathe my censure
What he might be. If what he might he is not,
270 I would to heaven he were.

Lodovico

What! Strike his wife!

Iago

Faith, that was not so well; yet would I knew
That stroke would prove the worst.

Lodovico

Is it his use?

Or did the letters work upon his blood
And new-create this fault?

---

250 *turn*: a) turn back; b) change allegiance (or brothel customer).

253 *obedient*: yielding (with sexual innuendo).
254 *proceed . . . tears*: carry on crying.
255 *well-painted passion*: a good show of grief.
257 *mandate*: command.
258 *avaunt*: get out of my sight.

259 *place*: position.
260 *sup*: eat supper.
261 *Goats and monkeys*: lecherous beasts; Othello's passion breaks through his self-control.

262 *full*: wise.
263 *all-in-all sufficient*: totally competent.
264 *solid*: steady.
265 *shot of accident*: cannon shot of fortune.
dart of chance: arrow of fate.

267 *his wits safe*: in his right mind.
light of brain: going insane.
268 *that*: what.
breathe my censure: give my opinion.
269–70 *If . . . were*: if he is not out of his mind, I wish to God he were (because nothing else could excuse his actions).

272 *use*: custom.
273 *work . . . blood*: anger him.

Iago

Alas, alas!

275 It is not honesty in me to speak
What I have seen and known. You shall observe him,
And his own courses will denote him so,
That I may save my speech. Do but go after,
And mark how he continues.

Lodovico

280 I am sorry that I am deceiv'd in him.   [*Exeunt*

277 *courses*: actions.
   denote: reveal.

SCENE 2

Othello's lodgings: enter Othello *and* Emilia

Othello
You have seen nothing then?
Emilia
Nor ever heard, nor ever did suspect.
Othello
Yes, you have seen Cassio and she together.
Emilia
But then I saw no harm, and then I heard
5 Each syllable that breath made up between them.
Othello
What! Did they never whisper?
Emilia

Never, my lord.
Othello
Nor send you out o'th'way?
Emilia

Never.
Othello
To fetch her fan, her gloves, her mask, nor nothing?
Emilia
Never, my lord.
Othello
10 That's strange.
Emilia
I durst, my lord, to wager she is honest,
Lay down my soul at stake. If you think other,
Remove your thought; it doth abuse your bosom.

Act 4 Scene 2
Othello questions Emilia, but refuses to
believe what he is told and confronts
Desdemona with his suspicions.
Desdemona turns to Iago for reassurance,
and Roderigo returns to reproach him for
unfair dealing; Iago promises them both
that all will be well.

15 *the serpent's curse*: 'Then the Lord
   God said to the serpent, Because thou
   hast done this [betrayed Adam and
   Eve], thou art cursed above all cattle,
   and above every beast of the field'
   (Genesis 3:14).
17 *happy*: fortunate.

19 *she's . . . bawd*: it would be a foolish
   brothel-keeper.
20 *This*: i.e. Desdemona.
21 *closet . . . key*: keeper of secrets.

26 *of your function*: with your job (i.e. as
   brothel-keeper).
27 *procreants*: those engaged in
   procreation.
29 *mystery*: trade.
   dispatch: get on with it.

If any wretch have put this in your head,
15 Let heaven requite it with the serpent's curse!
For if she be not honest, chaste, and true,
There's no man happy. The purest of their wives
Is foul as slander.
    Othello
            Bid her come hither; go!
                    [*Exit* Emilia
She says enough; yet she's a simple bawd
20 That cannot say as much. This is a subtle whore,
A closet lock and key of villainous secrets;
And yet she'll kneel and pray. I have seen her do't.

    Enter Desdemona *and* Emilia

    Desdemona
My lord, what is your will?
    Othello
              Pray, chuck, come hither.
    Desdemona
What is your pleasure?
    Othello
           Let me see your eyes.
25 Look in my face.
    Desdemona
         What horrible fancy's this?
    Othello
[*To* Emilia] Some of your function, mistress:
Leave procreants alone and shut the door;
Cough or cry 'hem' if anybody come.
Your mystery, your mystery! Nay, dispatch!
                    [*Exit* Emilia
    Desdemona
30 Upon my knees, what doth your speech import?
I understand a fury in your words,
But not the words.
    Othello
        Why? What art thou?
    Desdemona
Your wife, my lord; your true and loyal wife.

Othello
Come, swear it; damn thyself;

35 | *like one of heaven*: like an angel.

35 Lest, being like one of heaven, the devils themselves
Should fear to seize thee. Therefore be double-damn'd:
Swear thou art honest.
    Desdemona
                      Heaven doth truly know it.
    Othello
Heaven truly knows that thou art false as hell.
    Desdemona
To whom, my lord? With whom? How am I false?
    Othello
40 Ah, Desdemon, away, away, away!
    Desdemona
Alas, the heavy day! Why do you weep?
Am I the motive of these tears, my lord?
If haply you my father do suspect
An instrument of this your calling back,
45 Lay not your blame on me. If you have lost him,
I have lost him too.
    Othello
                  Had it pleas'd heaven
To try me with affliction, had they rain'd
All kind of sores and shames on my bare head,
Steep'd me in poverty to the very lips,
50 Given to captivity me and my utmost hopes,
I should have found in some place of my soul
A drop of patience. But, alas, to make me
The fixed figure for the time of scorn
To point his slow unmoving finger at!
55 Yet could I bear that too, well, very well;
But there where I have garner'd up my heart,
Where either I must live or bear no life,
The fountain from the which my current runs
Or else dries up—to be discarded thence
60 Or keep it as a cistern for foul toads
To knot and gender in! Turn thy complexion there,
Patience, thou young and rose-lipp'd cherubin;
Ay, there look grim as hell!
    Desdemona
I hope my noble lord esteems me honest.

41 | *heavy*: sorrowful.
42 | *motive*: cause.
43 | *haply*: by chance.

45 | *him*: his favour.

46 | *Had it*: if it had.
47 | *try*: test.

49 | *Steep'd*: submerged.
50 | *utmost*: all.

53 | *fixed*: fixèd.
53–4 | *The . . . at*: an eternal object of derision pointed at like the numbers on a clock-face.
56 | *garner'd*: stored.

58 | *fountain*: source.
     current: stream.

60 | *cistern*: water-tank.

61 | *knot and gender*: copulate and engender.
62 | *cherubin*: angel.

64 | *esteems*: considers.
     honest: chaste.

65 *shambles*: slaughterhouses.

66 *quicken . . . blowing*: hatch as soon as the eggs are laid.

72 *commoner*: common whore.

73 *forges*: furnaces.

76 *it*: the smell.
 winks: closes its eye.

78 *hollow mine*: depths, bowels.

82 *vessel*: i.e. her body; the expression is biblical.

87 *cry you mercy*: beg your pardon.

88 *took you for*: mistook you for.

Othello

65 O ay: as summer flies are in the shambles,
That quicken even with blowing. O, thou weed,
Who art so lovely fair and smell'st so sweet
That the sense aches at thee, would thou hadst ne'er
    been born!

Desdemona

Alas, what ignorant sin have I committed?

Othello

70 Was this fair paper, this most goodly book,
Made to write 'whore' upon? What committed!
Committed! O thou public commoner!
I should make very forges of my cheeks
That would to cinders burn up modesty

75 Did I but speak thy deeds. What committed!
Heaven stops the nose at it, and the moon winks;
The bawdy wind, that kisses all it meets,
Is hush'd within the hollow mine of earth
And will not hear it. What committed?

80 Impudent strumpet!

Desdemona

                            By heaven, you do me wrong.

Othello

Are not you a strumpet?

Desdemona

                              No, as I am a Christian.
If to preserve this vessel for my lord
From any other foul unlawful touch
Be not to be a strumpet, I am none.

Othello

85 What, not a whore?

Desdemona

                          No, as I shall be sav'd.

Othello

Is't possible?

Desdemona

O, heaven forgive us!

Othello

                        I cry you mercy then:
I took you for that cunning whore of Venice

That married with Othello. You, mistress,
90 That have the office opposite to Saint Peter,
And keeps the gate of hell! You, you, ay, you!

Enter Emilia

We have done our course; there's money for your
    pains.
I pray you turn the key, and keep our counsel.   [*Exit*

Emilia
Alas, what does this gentleman conceive?
95 How do you, madam? How do you, my good lady?

Desdemona
Faith, half-asleep.

Emilia
Good madam, what's the matter with my lord?

Desdemona
With who?

Emilia
Why, with my lord, madam.

Desdemona
100 Who is thy lord?

Emilia
            He that is yours, sweet lady.

Desdemona
I have none. Do not talk to me, Emilia.
I cannot weep, nor answers have I none
But what should go by water. Prithee tonight
Lay on my bed my wedding sheets, remember;
105 And call thy husband hither.

Emilia
            Here's a change indeed!
                           [*Exit*

Desdemona
'Tis meet I should be us'd so, very meet!
How have I been behav'd that he might stick
The smallest opinion on my least misuse?

90–1 *have . . . hell*: 'Her [the harlot's] house is the way to hell, going down unto the chambers of death.' (Proverbs 7:27).

90 *Saint Peter*: The saint who guards the gates of heaven.

92 *done our course*: finished our business (with sexual overtones).

93 *turn the key*: unlock the door (Emilia was told to close the door at line 27). *keep our counsel*: keep quiet about what we have been doing.

94 *conceive*: imagine.

96 *half-asleep*: Desdemona is dazed by Othello's words.

103 *go by water*: be conveyed by tears.

106 *meet*: fitting; Desdemona is perhaps bitterly ironical, rather than meekly submissive.

107 *How . . . behav'd*: What have I done?

107–8 *that . . . misuse*: to give him any reason for misinterpreting my smallest fault.

Enter Iago *and* Emilia

Iago
What is your pleasure, madam? How is't with you?
Desdemona
110 I cannot tell. Those that do teach young babes
Do it with gentle means and easy tasks.
He might have chid me so; for, in good faith,
I am a child to chiding.
Iago
                    What is the matter, lady?
Emilia
Alas, Iago, my lord hath so bewhor'd her,
115 Thrown such despite and heavy terms upon her
As true hearts cannot bear.
Desdemona
Am I that name, Iago?
Iago
                    What name, fair lady?
Desdemona
Such as she said my lord did say I was.
Emilia
He call'd her whore. A beggar in his drink
120 Could not have laid such terms upon his callet.
Iago
Why did he so?
Desdemona
I do not know; I am sure I am none such.
Iago
Do not weep, do not weep! Alas the day!
Emilia
Hath she forsook so many noble matches,
125 Her father, and her country, and her friends,
To be call'd whore? Would it not make one weep?
Desdemona
It is my wretched fortune.
Iago
                    Beshrew him for't!
How comes this trick upon him?
Desdemona
                    Nay, heaven doth know.

113 *a child to chiding*: unaccustomed to being scolded.

114 *bewhor'd her*: called her a whore.
115 *despite and heavy terms*: contempt and insults.

119 *in his drink*: drunken.
120 *laid such terms*: used such language.
    callet: slut.

124 *forsook*: given up.

127 *Beshrew*: curse.
128 *trick*: delusion.

129 *eternal*: damned (eternally); without knowing, Emilia describes her husband.
130 *busy*: interfering.
131 *cogging*: lying.
cozening: cheating.
to get some office: for some reason, *or* to get some job out of it; Emilia is very close to the truth.
133 *impossible*: Iago listens to the descriptions of his villainy while denying its possibility.
135 *A halter pardon him*: may he be hanged.
136 *keeps her company*: is her lover.

137 *form*: appearance.
what likelihood?: what grounds for such an inference?
139 *scurvy*: miserable.
140 *companions*: villains.
thou'dst: thou wouldest; i.e. I wish you would.
unfold: reveal.

143 *within door*: quietly.

144 *squire*: fellow.
145 *seamy side without*: wrong side out.
146 *suspect me*: i.e. of adultery.

151–8 Desdemona prays that she may lose all peace of body and soul if she ever sinned or sins against Othello.
151 *will*: wishes.
trespass: offend.
152 *discourse of thought*: process of thinking.
154 *Delighted them*: enjoyed.

158 *Comfort forswear me*: May all happiness forsake me.

Emilia
I will be hang'd if some eternal villain,
130 Some busy and insinuating rogue,
Some cogging, cozening slave, to get some office,
Have not devis'd this slander; I'll be hang'd else.
    Iago
Fie, there is no such man; it is impossible.
    Desdemona
If any such there be, heaven pardon him.
    Emilia
135 A halter pardon him and hell gnaw his bones!
Why should he call her whore? Who keeps her
    company?
What place, what time, what form, what likelihood?
The Moor's abus'd by some most villainous knave,
Some base notorious knave, some scurvy fellow.
140 O heaven, that such companions thou'dst unfold,
And put in every honest hand a whip
To lash the rascals naked through the world,
Even from the east to th'west!
    Iago
                                Speak within door.
    Emilia
O fie upon them! Some such squire he was
145 That turn'd your wit the seamy side without
And made you to suspect me with the Moor.
    Iago
You are a fool, go to.
    Desdemona
                O good Iago,
What shall I do to win my lord again?
Good friend, go to him; for, by this light of heaven,
150 I know not how I lost him. Here I kneel:
If e'er my will did trespass 'gainst his love
Either in discourse of thought or actual deed;
Or that mine eyes, mine ears, or any sense
Delighted them in any other form;
155 Or that I do not yet, and ever did,
And ever will—though he do shake me off
To beggarly divorcement—love him dearly,
Comfort forswear me! Unkindness may do much,

159 *defeat*: destroy.

161 *abhor*: a) disgust; b) make me a
      whore.
162 *addition*: title.
163 *vanity*: (useless) finery.

164 *but his humour*: only his mood.
165 *does him offence*: annoys him.
166 *chide with you*: quarrel with you.

167 *no other*: nothing else.

169 *stay the meat*: await the meal.

174 *daff'st . . . device*: put me off with
      some excuse.

176 *conveniency*: opportunity.

178 *put up*: endure.

182 *no kin together*: bear no relation to
      each other.

And his unkindness may defeat my life,

160 But never taint my love. I cannot say 'whore':
It does abhor me now I speak the word;
To do the act that might the addition earn
Not the world's mass of vanity could make me.
        Iago
I pray you be content; 'tis but his humour.
165 The business of the state does him offence,
And he does chide with you.
        Desdemona
If 'twere no other—
        Iago
                          It is but so, I warrant.

Trumpets sound within

Hark how these instruments summon to supper!
The messengers of Venice stay the meat.
170 Go in, and weep not; all things shall be well.
                    [*Exeunt* Desdemona *and* Emilia

Enter Roderigo

How now, Roderigo?
        Roderigo
I do not find that thou deal'st justly with me.
        Iago
What in the contrary?
        Roderigo
Every day thou daff'st me with some device, Iago, and
175 rather, as it seems to me now, keep'st from me all
conveniency than suppliest me with the least advantage
of hope. I will indeed no longer endure it. Nor am I yet
persuaded to put up in peace what already I have
foolishly suffered.
        Iago
180 Will you hear me, Roderigo?
        Roderigo
Faith, I have heard too much; for your words and
performances are no kin together.

Iago

You charge me most unjustly.

Roderigo

With naught but truth. I have wasted myself out of my
185 means. The jewels you have had from me to deliver to
Desdemona would half have corrupted a votarist. You
have told me she hath received them, and returned me
expectations and comforts of sudden respect and
acquaintance, but I find none.

Iago

190 Well, go to; very well.

Roderigo

Very well, go to! I cannot go to, man, nor 'tis not very
well. By this hand, I say 'tis very scurvy and begin to
find myself fopped in it.

Iago

Very well.

Roderigo

195 I tell you 'tis not very well. I will make myself known to
Desdemona. If she will return me my jewels, I will give
over my suit and repent my unlawful solicitation; if not,
assure yourself I will seek satisfaction of you.

Iago

You have said now?

Roderigo

200 Ay, and said nothing but what I protest intendment of
doing.

Iago

Why, now I see there's mettle in thee, and even from this
instant do build on thee a better opinion than ever
before. Give me thy hand, Roderigo. Thou hast taken
205 against me a most just exception; but yet I protest I have
dealt most directly in thy affair.

Roderigo

It hath not appeared.

Iago

I grant indeed it hath not appeared; and your suspicion
is not without wit and judgement. But, Roderigo, if
210 thou hast that in thee indeed, which I have greater
reason to believe now than ever—I mean purpose,

---

183 *charge*: accuse.

184–5 *wasted . . . means*: ruined myself
financially.

186 *half*: easily.
votarist: nun.

188 *comforts*: encouragement.
sudden respect: immediate attention.

193 *fopped*: fooled.

197 *solicitation*: courtship.
198 *seek satisfaction*: demand repayment.

199 *You . . . now?*: have you spoken your
mind?

200 *protest intendment*: declare an
intention.

202 *mettle*: spirit.
203 *build . . . opinion*: think better of you.
204–5 *taken . . . exception*: made a very
reasonable objection.
205 *protest*: declare.
206 *directly . . . affair*: honestly in your
interests.

207 It doesn't look that way.

214–15 *engines for my life*: plots against my life.

216 *compass*: possibility.

221 *Mauritania*: part of Western Africa (but perhaps a ruse to make Roderigo think that he will lose Desdemona).
222 *abode*: stay (in Cyprus).
lingered: delayed.
223 *determinate*: certain.

230 *harlotry*: little whore.
231 *his honourable fortune*: i.e. that he has been made Othello's deputy in Cyprus.
232 *going thence*: leaving there.
fashion: organize.
fall out: take place.
234 *second*: support.
236 *necessity in*: need for.
237–8 *put it on him*: bring about his death.
238 *high*: fully.
238–9 *grows to waste*: is getting late.
239 *About it*: get on with it.

courage, and valour—this night show it. If thou the next night following enjoy not Desdemona, take me from this world with treachery, and devise engines for
215 my life.
    Roderigo
Well, what is it? Is it within reason and compass?
    Iago
Sir, there is especial commission come from Venice to depute Cassio in Othello's place.
    Roderigo
Is that true? Why, then Othello and Desdemona return
220 again to Venice.
    Iago
O no, he goes into Mauritania and takes away with him the fair Desdemona, unless his abode be lingered here by some accident; wherein none can be so determinate as the removing of Cassio.
    Roderigo
225 How do you mean 'removing' of him?
    Iago
Why, by making him uncapable of Othello's place—knocking out his brains.
    Roderigo
And that you would have me to do?
    Iago
Ay, if you dare do yourself a profit and a right. He sups
230 tonight with a harlotry, and thither will I go to him. He knows not yet of his honourable fortune. If you will watch his going thence—which I will fashion to fall out between twelve and one—you may take him at your pleasure. I will be near to second your attempt, and he
235 shall fall between us. Come, stand not amazed at it, but go along with me. I will show you such a necessity in his death that you shall think yourself bound to put it on him. It is now high supper-time and the night grows to waste. About it!
    Roderigo
240 I will hear further reason for this.
    Iago
And you shall be satisfied.   [*Exeunt*

Act 4 Scene 3
Desdemona prepares for bed as her
husband walks home with his guests.

SCENE 3

Desdemona's *bedchamber; enter* Othello, Lodovico,
Desdemona, Emilia, *and* Attendants

Lodovico
I do beseech you, sir, trouble yourself no further.
Othello
O, pardon me; 'twill do me good to walk.
Lodovico
Madam, good night. I humbly thank your ladyship.
Desdemona
Your honour is most welcome.
Othello
5 Will you walk, sir? O, Desdemona.
Desdemona
My lord?
Othello

7 *on th'instant*: at once.

8 *forthwith*: immediately.
Dismiss: Usually the maid would stay
with her mistress until the husband
was ready for bed.

Get you to bed on th'instant. I will be returned
forthwith. Dismiss your attendant there. Look't be
done.
Desdemona
10 I will, my lord.
                    [*Exeunt* Othello, Lodovico, *and* Attendants
Emilia
How goes it now? He looks gentler than he did.
Desdemona

12 *incontinent*: straight away.

He says he will return incontinent;
He hath commanded me to go to bed
And bade me to dismiss you.
Emilia
                              Dismiss me?
Desdemona
15 It was his bidding; therefore, good Emilia,

16 *nightly wearing*: night clothes.

Give me my nightly wearing, and adieu.
We must not now displease him.
Emilia
I would you had never seen him.
Desdemona

19 *So . . . I*: that is not my wish.
approve: value; Desdemona's love has
not changed, despite Othello's harsh
words.
20 *checks*: rebukes.

So would not I: my love doth so approve him
20 That even his stubbornness, his checks, his frowns—

22 *those sheets*: i.e. the wedding sheets.

23 *All's one*: it doesn't matter;
Desdemona seems to have forgotten
the romantic hope that she could
reconcile Othello.

24 *shroud me*: It was customary to save
one of the best sheets to wrap the
dead body before burial.

25 *you talk*: you're talking nonsense.

26 *Barbary*: an old form of 'Barbara'.

28 *of willow*: the willow tree was the
emblem of forsaken lovers.

31 *I have much to do*: I find it hard to
stop myself.

33 *dispatch*: hurry up.

34 *nightgown*: dressing-gown.

35 *proper*: good-looking; the two women
discuss the departed guest.

36 *speaks well*: talks interestingly.

38 *touch . . . lip*: a kiss.

39 *sycamore*: willow (emblem of rejected
love).

Prithee, unpin me—have grace and favour in them.

Emilia

I have laid those sheets you bade me on the bed.

Desdemona

All's one. Good faith, how foolish are our minds!
If I do die before thee, prithee shroud me
25 In one of those same sheets.

Emilia

                    Come, come, you talk.

Desdemona

My mother had a maid called Barbary:
She was in love, and he she lov'd prov'd mad
And did forsake her. She had a song of willow;
An old thing 'twas but it expressed her fortune,
30 And she died singing it. That song tonight
Will not go from my mind. I have much to do
But to go hang my head all at one side
And sing it like poor Barbary—prithee, dispatch.

Emilia

Shall I go fetch your nightgown?

Desdemona

                     No, unpin me here.

35 This Lodovico is a proper man.

Emilia

A very handsome man.

Desdemona

                He speaks well.

Emilia

I know a lady in Venice would have walked barefoot to
Palestine for a touch of his nether lip.

Desdemona

[*Sings*] The poor soul sat sighing by a sycamore tree,
40   Sing all a green willow;
    Her hand on her bosom, her head on her knee,
    Sing willow, willow, willow;
    The fresh streams ran by her and murmur'd
        her moans;
    Sing willow, willow, willow.
45   Her salt tears fell from her and soften'd the
        stones—

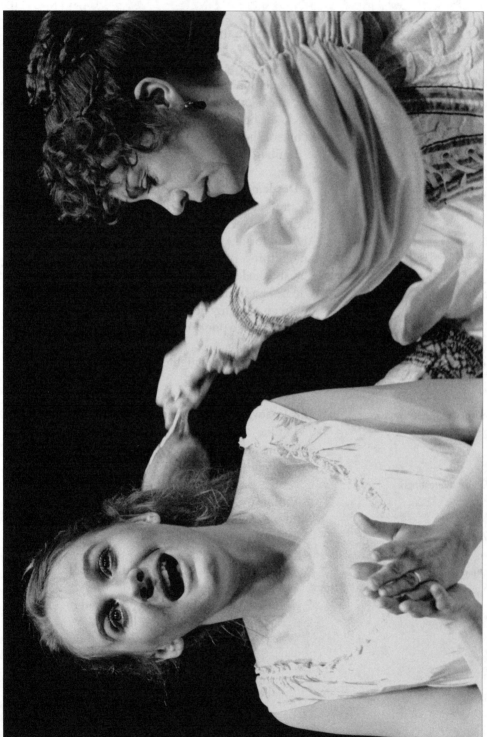

'The poor soul sat sighing by a sycamore tree' (4, 3, 39). Niamh Cusack as Desdemona and Janet Dale as Emilia, Royal Shakespeare Company, 1986.

46 *Lay by these*: put away these (i.e. her jewels).

48 *hie thee*: go away.
   anon: at once.

55 *moe*: an obsolete (poetic) form of 'more'.
   couch: sleep.

57 *bode*: foretell.

59 *in conscience*: honestly.

60 *abuse*: deceive.

61 *such gross kind*: i.e. by committing adultery.

63 *by . . . light*: by daylight.

68 *small vice*: Emilia dismisses the sin that is causing so much anguish to Othello and Desdemona.

Lay by these.
        Sing willow, willow, willow—
Prithee, hie thee; he'll come anon.
        Sing all a green willow must be my garland.
50   Let nobody blame him; his scorn I approve—
Nay that's not next. Hark, who is't that knocks?

Emilia
It's the wind.

Desdemona
[*Sings*] I call'd my love false love, but what said he
        then?
        Sing willow, willow, willow;
55   If I court moe women, you'll couch with moe
        men—
So get thee gone; good night. Mine eyes do itch—
Does that bode weeping?

Emilia
                        'Tis neither here nor there.

Desdemona
I have heard it said so. O, these men, these men!
Dost thou in conscience think—tell me, Emilia—
60 That there be women do abuse their husbands
In such gross kind?

Emilia
                        There be some such, no question.

Desdemona
Wouldst thou do such a deed for all the world?

Emilia
Why, would not you?

Desdemona
                        No, by this heavenly light.

Emilia
Nor I neither by this heavenly light;
65 I might do't as well i'th'dark.

Desdemona
Wouldst thou do such a deed for all the world?

Emilia
The world's a huge thing; it is a great price
For a small vice.

69 *undo't*: make it right.

70 *joint-ring*: a ring made in two separate parts.

71 *measures of lawn*: lengths of fabric.

72 *exhibition*: allowance of money.

73 *'Ud's*: God's (a censored form).

74–5 *venture purgatory*: risk being condemned to purgatory.

82 *to th'vantage*: in addition.

83 *store*: populate.

84 *But I do think*: This is the first time in the play that Emilia has been allowed to speak her real mind; Desdemona seems not to hear, being absorbed in her own troubled thoughts.

85 *fall*: sin.
   slack their duties: fail to perform their sexual obligations.

86 *pour . . . laps*: give what should be ours to strange women.

88 *Throwing . . . us*: Restricting our freedom.

89 *scant*: reduce.
   former having: what we used to have.
   in despite: out of spite.

90 *galls*: spirits capable of resentment.
   grace: i.e. to forgive them.

92 *sense*: feelings.

95 *sport*: for amusement.

96 *affection*: desire.

Desdemona

        In troth, I think thou wouldst not.

Emilia

In troth, I think I should, and undo't when I had done

70 it. Marry, I would not do such a thing for a joint-ring,
nor for measures of lawn, nor for gowns, petticoats, nor
caps, nor any petty exhibition. But for all the whole
world! Ud's pity, who would not make her husband a
cuckold, to make him a monarch? I should venture

75 purgatory for't.

Desdemona

Beshrew me, if I would do such a wrong for the whole
world.

Emilia

Why, the wrong is but a wrong i'th'world; and having
the world for your labour, 'tis a wrong in your own

80 world, and you might quickly make it right.

Desdemona

I do not think there is any such woman.

Emilia

Yes, a dozen; and as many to th'advantage as would
store the world they played for.
But I do think it is their husbands' faults

85 If wives do fall. Say that they slack their duties
And pour our treasures into foreign laps,
Or else break out in peevish jealousies,
Throwing restraint upon us; or say they strike us,
Or scant our former having in despite—

90 Why, we have galls, and though we have some grace,
Yet have we some revenge. Let husbands know
Their wives have sense like them: they see, and smell,
And have their palates both for sweet and sour
As husbands have. What is it that they do

95 When they change us for others? Is it sport?
I think it is. And doth affection breed it?
I think it doth. Is't frailty that thus errs?
It is so too. And have not we affections,
Desires for sport, and frailty, as men have?

100 *use us well*: treat us kindly.
101 *ills*: wrongs.
     instruct us so: teach us to do the
     same.
102 *Good night*: Throughout Emilia's
     worldly-wise soliloquy, Desdemona has
     been silent; now she articulates a
     quite different philosophy.
103 *pick*: learn.
     by bad mend: amend myself by
     learning from bad examples, *or* from
     my own suffering.

100 Then let them use us well; else let them know
     The ills we do, their ills instruct us so.
       Desdemona
     Good night, good night. God me such uses send,
     Not to pick bad from bad, but by bad mend! [*Exeunt*

ACT 5

Act 5 Scene 1
Roderigo and Iago lie in wait for Cassio; there is a struggle in which both Roderigo and Cassio are injured; Iago kills Roderigo after Othello, apparently approving his actions, has gone home to Desdemona.

1 *bulk*: projecting wall—which on the stage would have been represented by a pillar.
straight: immediately.
2 *bare*: unsheathed.
put it home: thrust it in deeply.
3 *at thy elbow*: near at hand, ready to help.
4 *makes . . . us*: Makes our fortunes, or else ruins us—a proverbial expression.
5 *resolution*: determination.
6 *miscarry*: make a mistake.

11 *young quat*: contemptible youngster (literally, a spot or pimple).
sense: quick— where it most hurts.
14 *makes my gain*: I win.
Live Roderigo: if Roderigo lives.
15 *calls me to*: demands from me.
large: full.
16 *bobb'd from him*: cheated him out of.
21 *unfold*: expose.
22 *soft*: hush.

SCENE 1

Outside Bianca's house: *enter* Iago *and* Roderigo

Iago
Here, stand behind this bulk, straight will he come.
Wear thy good rapier bare, and put it home.
Quick, quick, fear nothing; I'll be at thy elbow.
It makes us or it mars us; think on that,
5 And fix most firm thy resolution.
    Roderigo
Be near at hand; I may miscarry in't.
    Iago
Here, at thy hand; be bold, and take thy stand.

He retires

    Roderigo
I have no great devotion to the deed,
And yet he hath given me satisfying reasons.
10 'Tis but a man gone. Forth my sword! He dies!
    Iago
[*Aside*] I have rubb'd this young quat almost to the
        sense,
And he grows angry. Now, whether he kill Cassio,
Or Cassio him, or each do kill the other,
Every way makes my gain. Live Roderigo,
15 He calls me to a restitution large
Of gold and jewels that I bobb'd from him
As gifts to Desdemona.
It must not be. If Cassio do remain,
He hath a daily beauty in his life
20 That makes me ugly; and besides, the Moor
May unfold me to him—there stand I in much peril.
No, he must die. But soft, I hear him coming.

Enter Cassio

23 *gait*: footsteps.

Roderigo
I know his gait; 'tis he. Villain, thou diest!

He lunges at Cassio

Cassio
That thrust had been mine enemy indeed

25 *coat*: probably Cassio is wearing a
leather jerkin.
26 *make proof of*: test.

25 But that my coat is better than thou think'st.
I will make proof of thine.

He wounds Roderigo

Roderigo
                        O, I am slain!

Iago *wounds* Cassio *in the leg and exit*

Cassio
I am maim'd forever. Help, ho! Murder, murder!

27s.d. *above*: i.e. from the balcony above
the stage.

Enter Othello *above*

Othello
[*Aside*] The voice of Cassio: Iago keeps his word.
    Roderigo
O villain that I am!
    Othello

29 *even so*: Othello seems to mistake
Roderigo's voice for Cassio's.

[*Aside*]   It is even so.
    Cassio
30 O help, ho! Light! A surgeon!
    Othello
[*Aside*] 'Tis he. O brave Iago, honest and just,
That hast such noble sense of thy friend's wrong!

33 *Minion*: A term of abuse (or affection).
dear: beloved.
34 *unblest fate*: cursed end.
hies: is coming fast.
35 *blotted*: wiped out.

Thou teachest me. Minion, your dear lies dead,
And your unblest fate hies. Strumpet, I come!
35 Forth of my heart those charms, thine eyes, are blotted;
Thy bed, lust-stain'd, shall with lust's blood be spotted.
                              [*Exit* Othello

36s.d. *Gratiano*: He has just arrived from Venice with the news of Brabantio's death (see *5, 2, 203*).

37 *watch*: night-watchman.
passage: passers-by.

38 *mischance*: accident.
direful: in great distress.

42 *heavy*: dark.
43 *counterfeits*: imposters.
44 *in to the cry*: to the rescue; Lodovico and Gratiano are strangers in a foreign town, and their hesitation is understandable.

47 *one*: someone; Iago appears as though he has been roused from bed.

Enter Lodovico *and* Gratiano

Cassio
What, ho! No watch? No passage? Murder, murder!
Gratiano
'Tis some mischance; the cry is very direful.
Cassio
O, help!
Lodovico
40 Hark!
Roderigo
O, wretched villain!
Lodovico
Two or three groan. It is a heavy night.
These may be counterfeits: let's think't unsafe
To come in to the cry without more help.
Roderigo
45 Nobody come? Then I shall bleed to death.
Lodovico
Hark!

Enter Iago, *with a light*

Gratiano
Here's one comes in his shirt, with light and weapons.
Iago
Who's there? Whose noise is this that cries on murder?
Lodovico
We do not know.
Iago
                          Did you not hear a cry?
Cassio
50 Here, here; for heaven's sake, help me!
Iago
                                    What's the matter?
Gratiano
This is Othello's ancient, as I take it.
Lodovico
The same indeed, a very valiant fellow.
Iago
What are you here that cry so grievously?

Cassio

Iago? O, I am spoil'd, undone by villains!

54 *spoil'd*: wounded.
undone: injured.

55 Give me some help.

Iago

O me, lieutenant! What villains have done this?

Cassio

I think that one of them is hereabout

And cannot make away.

58 *make away*: escape.

Iago

            O, treacherous villains!

[*To* Lodovico *and* Gratiano] What are you there?

Come in, and give some help.

Roderigo

60 O, help me here!

Cassio

That's one of them.

Iago

            O murderous slave! O villain!

He stabs Roderigo

Roderigo

O damn'd Iago! O inhuman dog!

He faints

Iago

Kill men i'th'dark? Where be these bloody thieves?

How silent is this town! Ho, murder, murder!

Lodovico *and* Gratiano *come forward*

65 What may you be? Are you of good or evil?

Lodovico

As you shall prove us, praise us.

66 Judge us (to be good or evil) when you
   know who we are.

Iago

Signior Lodovico?

Lodovico

He, sir.

Iago

69 *cry you mercy*: beg your pardon.

I cry you mercy. Here's Cassio hurt by villains.

Gratiano

70 Cassio?

Iago

How is't, brother?

Cassio

My leg is cut in two.

Iago

                              Marry, heaven forbid!

Light, gentlemen. I'll bind it with my shirt.

Enter Bianca

Bianca

What is the matter, ho? Who is't that cried?

Iago

75 Who is't that cried?

Bianca

O, my dear Cassio, my sweet Cassio!

O, Cassio, Cassio, Cassio!

Iago

O notable strumpet! Cassio, may you suspect

Who they should be that have thus mangl'd you?

Cassio

80 No.

Gratiano

I am sorry to find you thus; I have been to seek you.

Iago

Lend me a garter: so. O for a chair

To bear him easily hence!

Bianca

                              Alas, he faints!

O, Cassio, Cassio, Cassio!

Iago

85 Gentlemen all, I do suspect this trash

To be a party in this injury.

Patience awhile, good Cassio. Come, come,

Lend me a light. Know we this face or no?

Alas, my friend and my dear countryman!

90 Roderigo? No—yes, sure—O, heaven, Roderigo!

Gratiano

What, of Venice?

78 *may you suspect*: can you guess?
79 *mangl'd*: wounded.

82 *garter*: Either a man or a woman could supply this—to fix the bandage made with Iago's shirt.

85 *trash*: Iago insults Bianca.
86 *be a party*: have a share in.

Iago
Even he, sir; did you know him?
Gratiano
                                        Know him? Ay.
Iago
Signior Gratiano! I cry your gentle pardon.
These bloody accidents must excuse my manners
95 That so neglected you.
Gratiano
                                        I am glad to see you.
Iago
How do you, Cassio? O, a chair, a chair!
Gratiano
Roderigo?
Iago
He, he, 'tis he.

Enter Attendants *with a chair*

98 *said*: done.

                                    O, that's well said, the chair!
Some good men bear him carefully from hence.
100 I'll fetch the general's surgeon. [*To* Bianca] For you,
      mistress,

101 *Save you your labour*: Stop interfering.

Save you your labour.—He that lies slain here, Cassio,
Was my dear friend. What malice was between you?
Cassio
None in the world, nor do I know the man.
Iago
[*To* Bianca] What, look you pale?—O, bear him out
      o'th'air.

Cassio is carried off; Roderigo's body is removed

105 Stay you, good gentleman. Look you pale, mistress?

106 *gastness*: look of terror.

Do you perceive the gastness of her eye?
[*To* Bianca] Nay, if you stare, we shall hear more anon.
Behold her well; I pray you, look upon her.
Do you see, gentlemen? Nay, guiltiness
110 Will speak, though tongues were out of use.

Enter Emilia

Emilia
'Las, what's the matter? What's the matter, husband?
Iago
Cassio hath here been set on in the dark

113 *'scap'd*: escaped.

By Roderigo and fellows that are 'scap'd.
He's almost slain and Roderigo dead.
Emilia
115 Alas, good gentleman! Alas, good Cassio!
Iago
This is the fruits of whoring. Prithee, Emilia,

117 *know of*: find out from.

Go know of Cassio where he supp'd tonight.
[*To* Bianca] What, do you shake at that?
Bianca

119 *I therefore shake not*: I'm not afraid to say so.

He supp'd at my house, but I therefore shake not.
Iago

120 *charge*: order.

120 O, did he so? I charge you go with me.
Emilia
O, fie upon thee, strumpet!
Bianca
I am no strumpet, but of life as honest
As you that thus abuse me.
Emilia
                                         As I? Foh! Fie upon thee!
Iago

124 *dress'd*: have his wound attended to.

Kind gentlemen, let's go see poor Cassio dress'd.
125 Come, mistress, you must tell's another tale.
Emilia, run you to the citadel

127 *happ'd*: chanced.

And tell my lord and lady what hath happ'd.
Will you go on afore? [*Aside*] This is the night

129 *fordoes*: ruins.
quite: utterly.

That either makes me, or fordoes me quite.   [*Exeunt*

Act 5 Scene 2

Othello hurries home from the scene of the fight to find Desdemona asleep in bed. Although she asserts her innocence, he kills her—and the murder is discovered by Emilia, who denounces her husband for slander. The wounded Cassio is brought to the scene, and Othello asks for his pardon. Finally Othello is arrested by Lodovico—but, before he can be taken away, he has his own final act to perform. This long scene is beautifully constructed, intermingling speeches of powerful eloquence with simple straightforward dialogue.

Os.d. *Desdemona in bed*: Desdemona's bed would probably be pushed forward from the curtained 'inner acting area' under the balcony.

1 *the cause*: adultery—Othello tries to justify his intended course of action.

2 *it*: adultery.

4 *whiter . . . snow*: whiter than snow.

5 *monumental alabaster*: a translucent stone used in making monuments.

6 *betray*: deceive.

7 *the light*: a) the torch he carries; b) Desdemona's life.

8 *flaming minister*: i.e. the lamp in his hand.

10 *Should*: if.

11 *cunning'st*: most artful.
pattern of: model to be copied by.

12 *Promethean heat*: Some Greek legends tell how Prometheus stole fire from the gods to animate the clay figures he had modelled, thus creating the first human beings.

13 *relume*: rekindle.

SCENE 2

Desdemona's bedchamber: enter Othello, *with a light, and* Desdemona *in bed*

Othello

It is the cause, it is the cause, my soul:
Let me not name it to you, you chaste stars.
It is the cause. Yet I'll not shed her blood,
Nor scar that whiter skin of hers than snow
5 And smooth as monumental alabaster—
Yet she must die, else she'll betray more men.
Put out the light, and then put out the light:
If I quench thee, thou flaming minister,
I can again thy former light restore,
10 Should I repent me; but once put out thy light,
Thou cunning'st pattern of excelling nature,
I know not where is that Promethean heat
That can thy light relume. When I have pluck'd thy rose,
I cannot give it vital growth again;
15 It needs must wither. I'll smell it on the tree.

He kisses her

17 *sword*: the weapon for the execution of justice.

O balmy breath, that dost almost persuade
Justice to break her sword! One more, one more!
Be thus when thou art dead, and I will kill thee
And love thee after. One more, and this the last.
20 So sweet was ne'er so fatal. I must weep.
But they are cruel tears: this sorrow's heavenly—
It strikes where it doth love. She wakes.

21–2 *this sorrow's . . . love*: 'For whom the Lord loveth, he chasteneth' (Hebrews 12:6).

Desdemona
Who's there? Othello?
    Othello
                Ay, Desdemona.
    Desdemona
Will you come to bed, my lord?
    Othello
25 Have you pray'd tonight, Desdemon?
    Desdemona
                        Ay, my lord.
    Othello

26 *bethink*: remember.
27 *Unreconcil'd . . . grace*: not forgiven by God.
28 *Solicit*: ask pardon.
   straight: immediately.

If you bethink yourself of any crime
Unreconcil'd as yet to heaven and grace,
Solicit for it straight.
    Desdemona
Alack, my lord, what may you mean by that?
    Othello

30 *I will walk by*: i.e. he will allow Desdemona privacy for her confession.
31 *unprepared spirit*: unpreparèd; not prepared for heaven.
32 *forfend*: forbid.

30 Well, do it, and be brief: I will walk by:
I would not kill thy unprepared spirit;
No—heaven forfend!—I would not kill thy soul.
    Desdemona
Talk you of killing?
    Othello
                Ay, I do.
    Desdemona
                    Then heaven
Have mercy on me!
    Othello
                Amen, with all my heart!
    Desdemona

34 *Amen*: I wish it may be so; the usual ending for a Christian prayer.

35 If you say so, I hope you will not kill me.
    Othello
Hum!

37 *fatal*: terrible.

Desdemona
And yet I fear you, for you're fatal then
When your eyes roll so. Why I should fear I know not,
Since guiltiness I know not, but yet I feel I fear.

Othello
40 Think on thy sins.

40 *They are . . . you*: i.e. loving another human being more than God.

Desdemona
                              They are loves I bear to you.

Othello
Ay, and for that thou diest.

42 It is unnatural to kill someone for loving.
43 *nether*: bottom.
44 *very frame*: whole body.
45 *portents*: portènts; bad signs.
46 *do not point on*: are not directed at.

Desdemona
That death's unnatural that kills for loving.
Alas, why gnaw you so your nether lip?
Some bloody passion shakes your very frame:
45 These are portents; but yet I hope, I hope
They do not point on me.

Othello
                                        Peace, and be still!

Desdemona
I will so. What's the matter?

Othello
That handkerchief which I so lov'd and gave thee,
Thou gav'st to Cassio.

Desdemona
                              No, by my life and soul!
50 Send for the man and ask him.

Othello
                                        Sweet soul, take heed.
Take heed of perjury: thou art on thy death-bed.

Desdemona
Ay, but not yet to die.

Othello
                                        Yes, presently.

52 *presently*: at once.
53 *freely*: fully.
54 *article*: item of which she is accused.
55 *choke*: kill by strangling.
conception: suspicion; the imagery is confirmed in the next line.
56 *groan withal*: labour with; Othello's suspicions of Desdemona are causing pain like birth pangs.

Therefore confess thee freely of thy sin;
For to deny each article with oath
55 Cannot remove nor choke the strong conception
That I do groan withal. Thou art to die.

Desdemona
Then Lord have mercy on me!

Othello

I say, Amen.

Desdemona

And have you mercy too! I never did

Offend you in my life; never lov'd Cassio

60   But with such general warranty of heaven

As I might love. I never gave him token.

Othello

By heaven, I saw my handkerchief in's hand.

O perjur'd woman! Thou dost stone my heart,

And mak'st me call what I intend to do

65   A murder, which I thought a sacrifice.

I saw the handkerchief.

Desdemona

He found it then;

I never gave it him. Send for him hither;

Let him confess a truth.

Othello

He hath confess'd.

Desdemona

What, my lord?

Othello

70   That he hath us'd thee.

Desdemona

How? Unlawfully?

Othello

Ay.

Desdemona

He will not say so.

Othello

No, his mouth is stopp'd:

Honest Iago hath tane order for't.

Desdemona

O, my fear interprets! What, is he dead?

Othello

75   Had all his hairs been lives, my great revenge

Had stomach for them all.

Desdemona

Alas, he is betray'd, and I undone.

60 *general warranty*: ordinary permission.

63 *stone my heart*: turn my heart to stone.
64–5 *And . . . sacrifice*: Desdemona's refusal to accept her guilt makes a murder of what Othello intended to be a sacrificial gesture.

67 *Send . . . hither*: order him to come here.

70 *us'd thee*: i.e. sexually.

72 *his mouth is stopp'd*: he has been silenced.
73 *tane order for't*: seen to it.

74 *my fear interprets*: I am afraid I understand.

75 *Had . . . lives*: If he had had as many lives as the hairs on his head.
76 *stomach*: appetite.

77 *undone*: ruined—but Othello understands this as an admission of guilt.

Othello

Out, strumpet! Weep'st thou for him to my face?

Desdemona

O banish me, my lord, but kill me not!

Othello

80 Down, strumpet!

Desdemona

Kill me tomorrow; let me live tonight!

Othello

Nay, if you strive—

Desdemona

But half an hour!

Othello

Being done, there is no pause.

Desdemona

But while I say one prayer!

Othello

It is too late.

Desdemona

85 O, Lord, Lord, Lord!

He smothers her

Emilia

[*Within*] My lord, my lord! What, ho! My lord, my lord!

Othello

What noise is this? Not dead? Not yet quite dead?

I that am cruel am yet merciful;

I would not have thee linger in thy pain.

90 So, so.

Emilia

[*Within*] What, ho! My lord, my lord!

Othello

Who's there?

Emilia

[*Within*] O, good my lord, I would speak a word with you.

Othello

Yes—'tis Emilia—by and by.—She's dead.

'Tis like she comes to speak of Cassio's death:

83 *Being . . . pause*: Now I have started, I must go on.

84 *But*: only.

93 *like*: likely.

94 *high*: loud.

<table>
<tr><td></td><td>The noise was high. Ha! No more moving?</td></tr>
<tr><td>95</td><td>Still as the grave. Shall she come in? Were't good?</td></tr>
</table>

The noise was high. Ha! No more moving?
95 Still as the grave. Shall she come in? Were't good?
I think she stirs again. No. What's best to do?
If she come in, she'll sure speak to my wife—
My wife, my wife! What wife? I have no wife.
O insupportable! O heavy hour!

99 *insupportable*: I can't bear it; Othello has begun to regret his deed.

101 *globe*: the whole world.

102 *yawn*: tear itself apart (in an earthquake). Othello is looking for the sort of confusion that might be associated with the end of the world. *alteration*: the change brought about by Desdemona's death.

100 Methinks it should be now a huge eclipse
Of sun and moon, and that th'affrighted globe
Should yawn at alteration.
    Emilia
[*Within*]   I do beseech you
That I may speak with you. O, good my lord!
    Othello
I had forgot thee. O, come in, Emilia.
105 Soft, by and by. Let me the curtains draw.
Where art thou?

He unlocks the door

                              What's the matter with thee now?

Enter Emilia

    Emilia
O, my good lord, yonder's foul murders done.
    Othello
What? Now?
    Emilia
But now, my lord.
    Othello

110–12 *It is . . . mad*: It was believed that the influence of the moon could turn people insane.
110 *error*: straying off course.
111 *was wont*: used to do.

110 It is the very error of the moon:
She comes more nearer earth than she was wont
And makes men mad.
    Emilia
Cassio, my lord, hath kill'd a young Venetian
Called Roderigo.
    Othello
                    Roderigo kill'd?
115 And Cassio kill'd?
    Emilia
                    No, Cassio is not kill'd.

116 *out of tune*: gone wrong.

Othello
Not Cassio kill'd! Then murder's out of tune,
And sweet revenge grows harsh.
  Desdemona
O, falsely, falsely murder'd!

118 *O falsely . . . murder'd*: Desdemona
revives momentarily.

  Emilia
         O Lord! What cry is that?
  Othello
That? What?
  Emilia
120 Out and alas, that was my lady's voice!

She draws the bed-curtains

Help, help, ho, help! O, lady, speak again!
Sweet Desdemona, O sweet mistress, speak!
  Desdemona
A guiltless death I die.
  Emilia
O, who hath done this deed?
  Desdemona
125 Nobody; I myself. Farewell.
Commend me to my kind lord. O farewell!

She dies

  Othello
Why, how should she be murder'd?
  Emilia
           Alas, who knows?
  Othello
You heard her say herself it was not I.
  Emilia
She said so; I must needs report the truth.
  Othello

130 *like a liar*: like the liar that she is.

130 She's like a liar gone to burning hell:
'Twas I that kill'd her.
  Emilia
        O, the more angel she,
And you the blacker devil!

133 *folly*: sin.

134 *belie*: lie about.

137 *top*: Othello picks up Iago's word
(3, 3, 397).

139 *But*: except.

140 *extremity*: final act.

144 *entire*: pure.
chrysolite: topaz (a semi-precious
stone); but the word may have been
chosen not for its meaning but
because of its sound.

149 *iterance*: repetition.

150 *made mocks with*: made a fool of.

Othello
She turned to folly, and she was a whore.
Emilia
Thou dost belie her, and thou art a devil.
Othello
135 She was false as water.
Emilia
                                    Thou art rash as fire to say
That she was false. O, she was heavenly true!
Othello
Cassio did top her: ask thy husband else.
O, I were damn'd beneath all depth in hell
But that I did proceed upon just grounds
140 To this extremity. Thy husband knew it all.
Emilia
My husband?
Othello
                    Thy husband.
Emilia
                                    That she was false to wedlock?
Othello
Ay, with Cassio. Nay, had she been true,
If heaven would make me such another world
Of one entire and perfect chrysolite,
145 I'd not have sold her for it.
Emilia
                                    My husband?
Othello
Ay, 'twas he that told me on her first;
An honest man he is, and hates the slime
That sticks on filthy deeds.
Emilia
                                    My husband?
Othello
What needs this iterance, woman? I say thy husband.
Emilia
150 O mistress, villainy hath made mocks with love!
My husband say that she was false?

Othello

He, woman;

I say thy husband. Dost understand the word?

My friend, thy husband, honest, honest Iago.

Emilia

If he say so, may his pernicious soul

155 Rot half a grain a day! He lies to th'heart.

She was too fond of her most filthy bargain.

Othello

Ha!

Emilia

Do thy worst.

This deed of thine is no more worthy heaven

160 Than thou wast worthy her.

Othello

Peace, you were best.

Emilia

Thou hast not half that power to do me harm

As I have to be hurt. O gull! O dolt!

As ignorant as dirt. Thou hast done a deed—

I care not for thy sword—I'll make thee known,

165 Though I lost twenty lives. Help! help! ho, help!

The Moor hath kill'd my mistress. Murder, murder!

Enter Montano, Gratiano, *and* Iago

Montano

What is the matter? How now, general?

Emilia

O, are you come, Iago? You have done well,

That men must lay their murders on your neck.

Gratiano

170 What is the matter?

Emilia

Disprove this villain, if thou be'st a man.

He says thou told'st him that his wife was false.

I know thou didst not, thou'rt not such a villain.

Speak, for my heart is full.

Iago

175 I told him what I thought, and told no more

Than what he found himself was apt and true.

---

155 *half a grain a day*: very, very slowly.
lies to th'heart: completely.

156 *too fond of*: infatuated with.
most filthy bargain: i.e. the husband for whom she paid such a high price.

159 *no more worthy heaven*: presumably Emilia means that the deed is damnable.

160 *Peace . . . best*: you had better shut up.

162 *to be hurt*: a) to endure anything you have the power to inflict; b) a capacity to feel pain on behalf of my mistress.
gull: fool.
dolt: idiot.

164 *I care . . . sword*: i.e. don't threaten me.

169 *lay . . . neck*: blame you for their murders.

176 *apt*: reasonable.

Emilia

But did you ever tell him she was false?

Iago

I did.

Emilia

179 *damned*: damnèd.

You told a lie, an odious damned lie:

180 Upon my soul, a lie, a wicked lie!

She false with Cassio? Did you say with Cassio?

Iago

182 *charm*: hold.

With Cassio, mistress. Go to, charm your tongue.

Emilia

I will not charm my tongue; I am bound to speak:

My mistress here lies murder'd in her bed.

All

185 O, heavens forfend!

Emilia

186 *set . . . on*: caused the murder.

And your reports have set the murder on.

Othello

Nay, stare not, masters; it is true indeed.

Gratiano

'Tis a strange truth.

Montano

O monstrous act!

Emilia

Villainy, villainy, villainy!

190 I think upon't, I think—I smell't—O villainy!

I thought so then; I'll kill myself for grief.

O villainy, villainy!

Iago

What, are you mad? I charge you get you home.

Emilia

Good gentlemen, let me have leave to speak.

195 *'Tis proper*: it is right; Elizabethans believed that wives should always obey their husbands.

195 'Tis proper I obey him, but not now.

Perchance, Iago, I will ne'er go home.

Othello

O! O! O!

Othello falls on the bed

197 *roar*: howl.

200 *scarce did know you, uncle*: hardly recognized you; Othello speaks to Gratiano, Desdemona's uncle and therefore (by marriage) his own.

204 *match*: marriage.
mortal: fatal.
205 *Shore . . . twain*: cut the thread of his life in two.
Did he live now: if he were alive now.
206 *turn*: deed.
207 He would drive away his guardian angel.
208 *reprobance*: a state of damnation.

210 *the act of shame*: adultery.

211 *a thousand times*: the expression is purely rhetorical, intended for emphasis not accuracy.
212 *gratify*: reward.
amorous works: love-making.
213 *recognizance*: token.
215 *antique*: ancient.
216 Shakespeare seems to have forgotten that in *Act 3*, Scene 4 Othello told Desdemona that the handkerchief was given to his mother by an Egyptian (lines 51–2).
O heavenly God: In the Folio text Emilia calls on the 'heavenly Powers'.

217 *'Twill out*: it [the truth] must come out.
I peace: must I keep quiet.
218 *liberal as the north*: as unrestrained as the north wind—a particularly violent and bitterly cold wind.

Emilia
       Nay, lay thee down and roar,
For thou hast kill'd the sweetest innocent
That e'er did lift up eye.
Othello
[*Standing up*]   O, she was foul!
200 I scarce did know you, uncle; there lies your niece,
Whose breath indeed these hands have newly stopp'd.
I know this act shows horrible and grim—
  Gratiano
Poor Desdemon, I am glad thy father's dead:
Thy match was mortal to him, and pure grief
205 Shore his old thread in twain. Did he live now,
This sight would make him do a desperate turn,
Yea, curse his better angel from his side
And fall to reprobance.
  Othello
'Tis pitiful; but yet Iago knows
210 That she with Cassio hath the act of shame
A thousand times committed. Cassio confess'd it,
And she did gratify his amorous works
With that recognizance and pledge of love
Which I first gave her. I saw it in his hand:
215 It was a handkerchief, an antique token
My father gave my mother.
  Emilia
         O God! O heavenly God!
Iago
Zounds, hold your peace!
  Emilia
        'Twill out, 'twill out. I peace!
No, I will speak as liberal as the north;
Let heaven, and men, and devils, let them all,
220 All, all cry shame against me, yet I'll speak.
  Iago
Be wise and get you home.
  Emilia
        I will not.

Iago *draws his sword and threatens* Emilia

Gratiano

                                                    Fie,

Your sword upon a woman!

    Emilia

O thou dull Moor, that handkerchief thou speak'st of

I found by fortune and did give my husband,

225 For often, with a solemn earnestness—

More than indeed belong'd to such a trifle—

He begg'd of me to steal it.

    Iago

                                                    Villainous whore!

    Emilia

She give it Cassio! No, alas, I found it

And I did give't my husband.

    Iago

                                                    Filth, thou liest!

    Emilia

230 By heaven, I do not, I do not, gentlemen.

O murderous coxcomb, what should such a fool

Do with so good a wife?

    Othello

                                        Are there no stones in heaven

But what serves for the thunder? Precious villain!

Othello runs at Iago; *Montano* disarms him; *Iago*
stabs Emilia *from behind and exit*

    Gratiano

The woman falls; sure he hath kill'd his wife.

    Emilia

235 Ay, ay; O, lay me by my mistress' side.

    Gratiano

He's gone, but his wife's kill'd.

    Montano

'Tis a notorious villain. Take you this weapon,

Which I have here recover'd from the Moor.

Come guard the door without; let him not pass,

240 But kill him rather. I'll after the same villain,

For 'tis a damned slave.

                                [*Exeunt* Montano *and* Gratiano

---

224 *by fortune*: by chance.

231 *coxcomb*: idiot.

232 *stones*: thunderbolts (to hurl at such villains).
233 *Precious*: A term used to intensify abuse.

237 *notorious*: absolute.

238 *recover'd from*: taken away from.

239 *without*: from the outside.
pass: get away.

241 *damned*: damnèd.

241 *I . . . neither*: Othello has lost the courage even to attack Iago.

242 *every . . . sword*: any novice fighter can defeat me.

243 *honour outlive honesty*: reputation last any longer than desert.

244 *bode*: foretell.

245–6 *play the swan . . . music*: Swans, which are mute, were fancied to sing only when they died.

248 *So . . . bliss*: may my soul be saved.

251 *a sword of Spain*: Toledo, in southern Spain, was famous for the manufacture of swords.
the ice-brook's temper: the steel was 'tempered' (= given its toughness) by being plunged into an icy stream.

254 *suffer*: get hurt.

256 *naked*: unarmed.

258 *sustain*: support.

262 *stop*: arrest.

264 *weapon'd*: armed.

265 *butt*: aim, goal.

Othello

                           I am not valiant neither,
But every puny whipster gets my sword.
But why should honour outlive honesty?
Let it go all.

   Emilia

                What did thy song bode, lady?

245 Hark, canst thou hear me? I will play the swan
And die in music: [*Sings*] 'Willow, willow, willow.'
Moor, she was chaste; she lov'd thee, cruel Moor;
So come my soul to bliss, as I speak true;
So speaking as I think, I die, I die.

She dies

Othello

250 I have another weapon in this chamber;
It was a sword of Spain, the ice-brook's temper.
O, here it is.—Uncle, I must come forth.

   Gratiano

[*Within*] If thou attempt it, it will cost thee dear;
Thou hast no weapon, and perforce must suffer.

   Othello

255 Look in upon me then, and speak with me,
Or naked as I am, I will assault thee.

Enter Gratiano

Gratiano
What is the matter?

   Othello

                    Behold, I have a weapon:
A better never did itself sustain
Upon a soldier's thigh. I have seen the day

260 That with this little arm and this good sword
I have made my way through more impediments
Than twenty times your stop. But, O vain boast!
Who can control his fate? 'Tis not so now.
Be not afraid, though you do see me weapon'd:

265 Here is my journey's end, here is my butt

'O Desdemon! Dead Desdemon! Dead! O! O!' (*5*, 2, 279) Ray Fearon as Othello and Zoe Waites as Desdemona, Royal Shakespeare Company, 2000.

266 *sea-mark*: beacon.
     utmost sail: last voyage.
267 *'Tis a lost fear*: There's nothing to be
     afraid of.
268 *Man*: aim.
     rush: reed.

270 *ill-starr'd*: ill-fated.
271 *smock*: a woman's under-garment.
     at compt: on the Day of Judgement.

274 *thy chastity*: Othello finally admits the
     truth.
275 *cursed*: cursèd.
     slave: Othello means himself.
275–8 *Whip . . . fire*: Othello visualizes
     some of the traditional medieval
     torturers in hell.
278 *steep-down*: precipitous.

283 *fable*: i.e. that a devil has cloven feet.

287 *in my sense*: as I feel now.

And very sea-mark of my utmost sail.
Do you go back dismay'd? 'Tis a lost fear:
Man but a rush against Othello's breast,
And he retires. Where should Othello go?

He goes to the bed

270 Now, how dost thou look now? O ill-starr'd wench!
Pale as thy smock! When we shall meet at compt
This look of thine will hurl my soul from heaven
And fiends will snatch at it. Cold, cold, my girl,
Even like thy chastity.
275 O cursed, cursed slave! Whip me, ye devils,
From the possession of this heavenly sight!
Blow me about in winds! Roast me in sulphur!
Wash me in steep-down gulfs of liquid fire!
O Desdemon! Dead Desdemon! Dead! O! O!

Enter Lodovico, Montano, Cassio *in a chair*, Iago *in
the charge of* Officers

Lodovico
280 Where is this rash and most unfortunate man?
Othello
That's he that was Othello: here I am.
Lodovico
Where is that viper? Bring the villain forth.
Othello
I look down towards his feet; but that's a fable.
If that thou be'st a devil, I cannot kill thee.

He wounds Iago

Lodovico
285 Wrench his sword from him.
Iago
                                    I bleed, sir, but not kill'd.
Othello
I am not sorry neither; I'd have thee live,
For in my sense 'tis happiness to die.

Lodovico

O, thou Othello, that wert once so good,

Fallen in the practice of a damned slave,

290 What shall be said to thee?

Othello

                                    Why, anything:

An honourable murderer, if you will;

For naught did I in hate, but all in honour.

Lodovico

This wretch hath part confess'd his villainy.

Did you and he consent in Cassio's death?

Othello

295 Ay.

Cassio

Dear general, I never gave you cause.

Othello

I do believe it, and I ask your pardon.

Will you, I pray, demand that demi-devil

Why he hath thus ensnar'd my soul and body?

Iago

300 Demand me nothing; what you know, you know.

From this time forth I never will speak word.

Lodovico

What! Not to pray?

Gratiano

Torments will ope your lips.

Othello

                                    Well, thou dost best.

Lodovico

Sir, you shall understand what hath befallen,

305 Which, as I think, you know not. Here is a letter

Found in the pocket of the slain Roderigo,

And here another: the one of them imports

The death of Cassio, to be undertook

By Roderigo.

Othello

              O villain!

Cassio

                                    Most heathenish and most gross!

289 *practice*: trap.

    damned: damnèd.

303 *Torments*: torture.

    thou dost best: you know best.

307 *imports*: concerns.

310 *discontented paper*: letter expressing dissatisfaction.

312 *damned*: damnèd.

313 *belike*: probably.
in the nick: just in time (a colloquial expression).
314 *Came in*: interposed.
satisfied him: gave him a satisfactory answer (by killing him).
315 *came you . . . by*: did you acquire?

317 *but even now*: only just now.

319 *wrought . . . desire*: worked in accordance with his wishes.

321 *upbraids*: reproaches.

322 *Brave*: challenge.
upon the watch: when I was on guard.
whereon it came: as a result of which.
323 *cast*: dismissed.
he: i.e. Roderigo.
325 *set him on*: incited him.
326 *forsake*: leave.

330 *hold him long*: make him suffer for a long time.
331 *close*: confined.

334 *Soft you*: wait a minute.

337 *unlucky*: unfortunate.
338 *nothing extenuate*: do not make excuses.

Lodovico
310 Now here's another discontented paper,
Found in his pocket too; and this, it seems,
Roderigo meant to have sent this damned villain,
But that, belike, Iago, in the nick,
Came in and satisfied him.
  Othello
                    O the pernicious caitiff!
315 How came you, Cassio, by that handkerchief
That was my wife's?
  Cassio
                    I found it in my chamber;
And he himself confess'd but even now
That there he dropp'd it for a special purpose
Which wrought to his desire.
  Othello
                    O fool, fool, fool!
  Cassio
320 There is besides in Roderigo's letter
How he upbraids Iago, that he made him
Brave me upon the watch, whereon it came
That I was cast; and even but now he spake—
After long seeming dead—Iago hurt him,
325 Iago set him on.
  Lodovico
You must forsake this room and go with us.
Your power and your command is taken off
And Cassio rules in Cyprus. For this slave,
If there be any cunning cruelty
330 That can torment him much and hold him long
It shall be his. You shall close prisoner rest
Till that the nature of your fault be known
To the Venetian state. Come, bring him away.
  Othello
Soft you; a word or two before you go.
335 I have done the state some service and they know't:
No more of that. I pray you, in your letters
When you shall these unlucky deeds relate,
Speak of me as I am; nothing extenuate,

339 *set down*: write.
340 *wisely*: i.e. moderately.
341 *wrought*: provoked.
342 *Perplex'd in the extreme*: completely bewildered.
343 *base*: low in rank, servile.
Indian: Many stories were told about the ignorance of Asian peoples and their non comprehension of Western values.
344 *subdued*: overcome (by grief).
345 *unused*: unusèd.
melting mood: weeping.
347 *medicinable gum*: myrrh (which oozed from certain Arabian trees, and was used in medical treatment and religious ceremonies).
350 *traduced*: betrayed.
351 *circumcised*: circumcisèd; i.e. Muhammedan.

353 *period*: conclusion.

357 *Spartan dog*: These were said to be always eager for prey.
358 *fell*: cruel.
359 *loading*: burden.
360 *object*: spectacle.
361 *Let it be hid*: The bed would now be drawn back into the recess under the balcony, and the curtains drawn.
keep: stay in.
362 *seize upon*: take legal possession of.
363 *succeed*: legally descend.
lord governor: i.e. Cassio.
364 *censure*: sentencing.

Nor set down aught in malice. Then must you speak
340 Of one that lov'd not wisely, but too well;
Of one not easily jealous but, being wrought,
Perplex'd in the extreme; of one whose hand,
Like the base Indian, threw a pearl away
Richer than all his tribe; of one whose subdued eyes,
345 Albeit unused to the melting mood,
Drops tears as fast as the Arabian trees
Their medicinable gum. Set you down this;
And say besides that in Aleppo once
Where a malignant and a turban'd Turk
350 Beat a Venetian and traduced the state,
I took by th'throat the circumcised dog
And smote him thus.

He stabs himself

Lodovico
O bloody period!
Gratiano
                    All that's spoke is marr'd!
Othello
I kiss'd thee ere I kill'd thee: no way but this,
355 Killing myself, to die upon a kiss.

He falls on the bed and dies

Cassio
This did I fear, but thought he had no weapon,
For he was great of heart.
Lodovico
[*To* Iago]   O Spartan dog,
More fell than anguish, hunger, or the sea,
Look on the tragic loading of this bed:
360 This is thy work. The object poisons sight;
Let it be hid. [*The bed-curtains are drawn*] Gratiano,
    keep the house
And seize upon the fortunes of the Moor,
For they succeed on you. To you, lord governor,
Remains the censure of this hellish villain:

365 The time, the place, the torture, O, enforce it!
Myself will straight aboard, and to the state
This heavy act with heavy heart relate.   [*Exeunt*

366–7 *Myself . . . relate*: The slow
formality of the rhymed couplet with
its sighing alliteration brings the play
to a solemn conclusion.

The 'Willow' Song

(Act 4, Scene 3)

Othello: *the Source*

This passage is taken from *Gli Hecatommithi* by Giovanni Battista Cinthio translated by Geoffrey Bullough (*Narrative and Dramatic Sources of Shakespeare*, Vol. VII, London, Routlege and Kegan Paul, 1973).

There was once in Venice a Moor, a very gallant man, who, because he was personally valiant and had given proof in warfare of great prudence and skilful energy, was very dear to the Signoria, who in rewarding virtuous actions ever advanced the interests of the Republic. It happened that a virtuous Lady of wondrous beauty called Disdemona, impelled not by female appetite but by the Moor's good qualities, fell in love with him, and he, vanquished by the Lady's beauty and noble mind, likewise was enamoured of her. So propitious was their mutual love that, although the Lady's relatives did all they could to make her take another husband, they were united in marriage and lived together in such concord and tranquillity while they remained in Venice, that never a word passed between them that was not loving.

It happened that the Venetian lords made a change in the forces that they used to maintain in Cyprus; and they chose the Moor as Commandant of the soldiers whom they sent there. Although he was pleased by the honour offered him . . . yet his happiness was lessened when he considered the length and dangers of the voyage, thinking that Disdemona would be much troubled by it. The Lady, who had no other happiness on earth but the Moor . . . could hardly wait for the hour when he would set off with his men, and she would accompany him to that honourable post . . . Shortly afterwards, having donned his armour and made all ready for the journey, he embarked in the galley with his lady, and with a sea of the utmost tranquillity arrived safely in Cyprus.

The Moor had in his company an Ensign of handsome presence but the most scoundrelly nature in the world. He was in high favour with the Moor, who had no suspicion of his wickedness; for although he had the basest of minds, he so cloaked the vileness hidden in his heart with high sounding and noble words, and by his manner, that he showed himself in the likeness of a Hector or an Achilles. This false man had likewise taken to Cyprus his wife, a fair and honest young woman. Being an Italian she was much loved by the Moor's wife, and spent the greater part of the day with her.

In the same company there was also a Corporal who was very dear to the Moor. This man went frequently to the Moor's house and often dined with him and his wife. The Lady, knowing him so well liked by her husband, gave him proofs of the greatest kindness, and this was much appreciated by the Moor.

The wicked Ensign, taking no account of the faith he had pledged to his wife, and of the friendship, loyalty and obligations he owed the Moor, fell ardently in love with Disdemona . . . He sought therefore in various ways, as deviously as he could, to make the Lady aware that he desired her. But she, whose every thought was for the Moor, never gave a thought to the Ensign . . . And all the things he did to arouse her feelings for him had no more effect than if he had not tried them. Whereupon he imagined that this was because she was in love with the Corporal, and he wondered how he might remove the latter from her sight. Not only did he turn his mind to this, but the love which he had felt for the Lady now changed to the bitterest hate, and he gave himself up to studying how to bring it about that, once the Corporal were killed, if he himself could not enjoy the Lady, then the Moor should not have her either. Turning over in his mind divers schemes, all wicked and treacherous, in the end he decided to accuse her of adultery, and to make her husband believe that the Corporal was the adulterer . . . Wherefore he set himself to wait until time and place opened a way for him to start his wicked enterprise.

Not long afterwards the Moor deprived the Corporal of his rank for having drawn his sword and wounded a soldier while on guard-duty. Disdemona was grieved by this and tried many times to reconcile the Moor with him. Whereupon the Moor told the rascally Ensign that his wife importuned him so much for the Corporal that he feared he would be obliged to reinstate him. The evil man saw in this a hint for setting in train the deceits he had planned, and said: 'Perhaps Disdemona has good cause to look on him so favourably!' 'Why is that?' asked the Moor. 'I do not wish,' said the Ensign, 'to come between man and wife, but if you keep your eyes open you will see for yourself.' Nor for all the Moor's inquiries would the Ensign go beyond this: nonetheless his words left such a sharp thorn in the Moor's mind, that he gave himself up to pondering intensely what they could mean. He became quite melancholy, and one day, when his wife was trying to soften his anger towards the Corporal, begging him not to condemn to oblivion the loyal service and friendship of many years just for one small fault, especially since the Corporal had been reconciled to the man he had struck, the Moor burst out in anger and said to her 'there must be a very powerful reason why you take such trouble for this fellow, for he is not your brother, nor even a kinsman, yet you have him so much at heart.

The Lady, all courtesy and modesty, replied: 'I should not like you to be angry with me ... Only a very good purpose made me speak to you about this, but rather than have you angry with me I shall never say another word on the subject.'

The Moor, however, seeing the earnestness with which his wife had again pleaded for the Corporal, guessed that the Ensign's words had been intended to suggest that Disdemona was in love with the Corporal, and he went in deep depression to the scoundrel and urged him to speak more openly. The Ensign, intent on injuring the unfortunate Lady, after pretending not to wish to say anything that might displease the Moor, appeared to be overcome by his entreaties and said: 'I must confess that it grieves me greatly to have to tell you something that must be in the highest degree painful to you; but since you wish me to tell you, and the regard that I must have of your honour as my master spurs me on, I shall not fail in my duty to answer your request. You must know therefore that it is hard for your Lady to see the Corporal in disgrace for the simple reason that she takes her pleasure with him whenever he comes to your house. The woman has come to dislike your blackness.'

These words struck the Moor's heart to its core; but in order to learn more (although he believed what the Ensign had said to be true, through the suspicion already sown in his mind) he said, with a fierce look: 'I do not know what holds me back from cutting out that outrageous tongue of yours which has dared to speak such insults against my Lady!' Then the Ensign: 'Captain,' he said, 'I did not expect any other reward for my loving service; but since my duty and my care for your honour have carried me so far, I repeat that the matter stands exactly as you have just heard it, and if your Lady with a false show of love for you, has so blinded your eyes that you have not seen what you ought to have seen, that does not mean that I am not speaking the truth. For this Corporal has told me all, like one whose happiness does not seem complete until he has made someone else acquainted with it.' And he added: 'If I had not feared your wrath, I should, when he told me, have given him the punishment he deserved by killing him. But since letting you know what concerns you more than anyone else brings me so undeserved a reward, I wish that I had kept silent, for by doing so I should not have fallen into your displeasure.'

Then the Moor, in the utmost anguish, said, 'If you do not make me see with my own eyes what you have told me, be assured, I shall make you realize that it would have been better for you had you been born dumb.'

[For some time the Ensign wondered what to do next, because 'his knowledge of the Lady's chastity' made it seem impossible that he should ever be able to make the Moor believe him; and then, 'his thoughts twisting and turning in all directions, the scoundrel thought of a new piece of mischief.']

The Moor's wife often went . . . to the house of the Ensign's wife, and stayed with her a good part of the day; wherefore seeing that she sometimes carried with her a handkerchief embroidered most delicately in the Moorish fashion, which the Moor had given her and which was treasured by the Lady and her husband too, the Ensign planned to take it from her secretly, and thereby prepare her final ruin. [One day, whilst Disdemona was playing with his child, the Ensign stole the handkerchief; he dropped it in the Corporal's room.]

[The Ensign] spoke to the Corporal one day while the Moor was standing where he could see them as they talked; and chatting of quite other matters than the Lady, he laughed heartily and, displaying great surprise, he moved his head about and gestured with his hands, acting as if he were listening to marvels. As soon as the Moor saw them separate he went to the Ensign to learn what the other had told him; and the Ensign, after making him entreat for a long time, finally declared: 'He has hidden nothing from me. He tells me that he has enjoyed your wife every time you have given them the chance by your absence, and on the last occasion she gave him the handkerchief which you gave her as a present when you married her.' The Moor thanked the Ensign and it seemed obvious to him that if he found that the Lady no longer had the handkerchief, then all must be as the Ensign claimed.

Wherefore one day after dinner . . . he asked her for this handkerchief. The unhappy woman, who had greatly feared this, grew red in the face at the request . . . 'I do not know,' she said, 'why I cannot find it.' . . .

Leaving her, the Moor began to think how he might kill his wife, and the Corporal too, in such a way that he would not be blamed for it. And since he was obsessed with this, day and night, the Lady inevitably noticed that he was not the same towards her as he was formerly. Many times she said to him, 'What is the matter with you? What is troubling you? Whereas you used to be the gayest of men, you are now the most melancholy man alive.'

The Moor invented various excuses, but she was not at all satisfied . . . Sometimes she would say to the Ensign's wife, 'I do not know what to make of the Moor. He used to be all love towards me, but in the last few days he has become quite another man; and I fear greatly that I shall be a warning to young girls not to marry against their parents' wishes; and Italian ladies will learn by my example not to tie themselves to a man whom Nature, Heaven, and the manner of life separate from us. But because I know that he is very friendly with your husband, and confides in him, I beg you, if you have learned anything from him which you can tell me, that you will not fail to help me.' She wept bitterly as she spoke . . .

The Corporal [who had recognized the handkerchief and tried, without success, to return it] had a woman at home who worked the most wonderful embroidery on lawn, and seeing the handkerchief and learning that it belonged to the Moor's wife, and that it was to be returned to her, she began to make a similar one before it went back. While she was doing so, the Ensign noticed that she was working near a window where she could be seen by whoever passed by on the street. So he brought the Moor and made him see her, and the latter now regarded it as certain that the most virtuous Lady was indeed an adulteress.

He arranged with the Ensign to kill her and the Corporal, and they discussed how it might be done. The Moor begged the Ensign to kill the Corporal, promising to remain eternally grateful to him. The Ensign refused to undertake such a thing, as being too difficult and dangerous, for the Corporal was as skilful as he was courageous; but after much entreaty, and being given a large sum of money, he was persuaded to say that he would tempt Fortune.

Soon after they had resolved on this, the Corporal, issuing one dark night from the house of a courtesan with whom he used to amuse himself, was accosted by the Ensign, sword in hand, who directed a blow at his legs to make him fall down; and he cut the right leg entirely through, so that the wretched man fell. The Ensign was immediately on him to finish him off, but the Corporal, who was valiant and used to blood and death, had drawn his sword, and wounded as he was he set about defending himself, while shouting in a loud voice: 'I am being murdered.'

At that the Ensign, hearing people come running . . . began to flee, so as not to be caught there; then, turning back he pretended to have run up on hearing the noise. Mingling with the others, and seeing the leg cut off, he judged that if the Corporal were not already dead, he soon would die of the wound, and although he rejoiced inwardly, he outwardly grieved for the Corporal as if he had been his own brother.

[Hearing of the Corporal's death, Disdemona grieved for him; but the Moor 'put the worst possible construction' on her grief. He plotted with the Ensign to murder her; they decided to use neither poison nor dagger, but to beat her to death with a stocking filled with sand and then pull down the ceiling to give the appearance of an accident. The Ensign hit her on the head, and Disdemona cried to the Moor for help, but he said]

'You wicked woman, you are having the reward of your infidelity. This is how women are treated who, pretending to love their husbands, put horns on their heads.'

The wretched Lady, hearing this and feeling herself near to death (for the Ensign had given her another blow), called on Divine Justice to witness her fidelity, since earthly justice failed, and she lay still, slain by the impious Ensign . . .

Next day Disdemona was buried, amid the universal mourning of the people. But God, the just observer of men's hearts, did not intend such vile wickedness to go without proper punishment. He ordained that the Moor, who had loved the Lady more than his life, on finding himself deprived of her should feel such longing that he went about like one beside himself, searching for her in every part of the house. Realizing now that the Ensign was the cause of his losing his Lady and all joy in life, he held the villain in such abhorrence that he could not bear even to see him; and if he had not been afraid of the inviolable justice of the Venetian lords, he would have slain him openly . . .

[The Ensign betrayed the plot, accusing the Moor of the murder, to the Captain, who told the Venetian authorities; the Moor was arrested, tortured and condemned to exile. Eventually he was murdered by Disdemona's relatives. The Ensign was later arrested, and 'tortured so fiercely that his inner organs were ruptured'; then he was sent home, 'where he died miserably'.]

It appeared marvellous to everybody that such malignity could have been discovered in a human heart; and the fate of the unhappy Lady was lamented, with some blame for her father . . . No less was the Moor blamed, who had believed too foolishly.

What the Critics have said

1. THOMAS RYMER, in the seventeenth century, seemed unable to respond to the poetry and passion of *Othello*, finding the action unreasonable and the characters incredible. He concluded an essay on the play with this judgement:

> There is in this play some burlesque, some humour and ramble of comical wit, some show and some mimicry to divert the spectators; but the tragical part is none other than a bloody farce, without salt or savour.
>
> *A Short View of Tragedy*, 1693

2. SAMUEL JOHNSON, the first of Shakespeare's great editors, had the highest praise for *Othello*:

> The beauties of this play impress themselves so strongly upon the attention of the reader, that they can draw no aid from critical illustration. The fiery openness of Othello, magnanimous, artless and credulous, boundless in his confidence, ardent in his affection, inflexible in his resolution, and obdurate in his revenge; the cool malignity of Iago, silent in his resentment, subtle in his designs, and studious at once of his interest and his vengeance; the soft simplicity of Desdemona, confident of merit, and conscious of innocence, her artless perseverance in her suit, and her slowness to suspect that she can be suspected, are such proofs of Shakespeare's skill in human nature, as, I suppose, it is vain to seek in any modern writer.
>
> General Remarks on *Othello*, 1765

3. S. T. COLERIDGE, at the beginning of the nineteenth century, was impressed above all by the character of Iago, whose explanatory soliloquies he saw as

> . . . the motive hunting of motiveless malignity—how awful! In itself fiendish; while yet he was allowed to bear the divine image, too fiendish for his own steady view. A being next to devil, only *not* quite devil—and this Shakespeare has attempted—and executed—without disgust, without scandal.
>
> Marginalia on *Othello*

4.　A. C. BRADLEY, at the beginning of the twentieth century, was fascinated by the character of Othello:

> Othello is, in one sense of the word, by far the most romantic figure among Shakespeare's heroes; and he is so partly from the strange life of war and adventure which he has lived from childhood. He does not belong to our world, and he seems to enter it we do not know whence—almost as if from wonderland. There is something mysterious in his descent from men of royal siege; in his wanderings in vast deserts and among marvellous peoples; in his tales of magic handkerchiefs and prophetic sibyls; in the sudden vague glimpses we get of numberless battles and sieges in which he has played the hero and has borne a charmed life; even in chance references to his baptism, his being sold to slavery, his sojourn in Aleppo.
>
> *Shakespearean Tragedy*, 1904

Background

England in 1604

When Shakespeare was writing *Othello*, many people still believed that the sun went round the earth. They were taught that this was the way God had ordered things, and that – in England – God had founded a Church and appointed a Monarchy so that the land and people could be well governed.

'The past is a foreign country; they do things differently there.'

L. P. Hartley

Government

For most of Shakespeare's life, the reigning monarch of England was Queen Elizabeth I. With her counsellors and ministers, she governed the nation from London, although fewer than half a million people out of a total population of six million lived in the capital city. In the rest of the country, law and order were maintained by the land-owners and enforced by their deputies. The average man had no vote, and women had no rights at all.

Religion

At this time, England was a Christian country. All children were baptized, soon after they were born, into the Church of England; they were taught the essentials of the Christian faith, and instructed in their duty to God and to humankind. Marriages and funerals were conducted only by the licensed clergy and according to the Church's rites and ceremonies. Attending divine service was compulsory; absences (without a good medical reason) could be punished by fines. By such means, the authorities were able to keep some control over the population – recording births, marriages, and deaths; being alert to anyone who refused to accept standard religious practices, who could be politically dangerous; and ensuring that people received the approved teachings through the official 'Homilies' which were regularly preached in all parish churches.

Elizabeth I's father, Henry VIII, had broken away from the Church of Rome, and from that time all people in England were able to hear the church services *in their own language* rather than in Latin. The Book of Common Prayer was used in every church, and an English translation of the Bible was read aloud in public. The Christian religion had never been so well taught before!

Education

School education reinforced the Church's teaching. From the age of four, boys might attend the 'petty school' (its name came from the French '*petite école*') to learn reading and writing along with a few prayers; some schools also included work with numbers. At the age of seven, boys were ready for the grammar schools (if their fathers were willing and able to pay the fees).

Grammar schools taught Latin grammar, translation work and the study of Roman authors, paying attention as much to style as to content. The art of fine writing was therefore important from early youth. A very few students went on to university; these were either clever boys who won scholarships, or else the sons of rich noblemen. Girls stayed at home, and learned domestic and social skills – cooking, sewing, perhaps even music. The lucky ones might learn to read and write.

Language

At the start of the sixteenth century the English had a very poor opinion of their own language: there was little serious writing in English, and hardly any literature. Latin was the language of international scholarship, and the eloquent style of the Romans was much admired. Many translations from Latin were made, and in this way writers increased the vocabulary of English and made its grammar more flexible. French, Italian, and Spanish works were also translated and, for the first time, there were English versions of the Bible. By the end of the century, English was a language to be proud of: it was rich in vocabulary, capable of infinite variety and subtlety, and ready for all kinds of word-play – especially *puns*, for which Elizabethan English is renowned.

Drama

The great art-form of the Elizabethan and Jacobean age was its drama. The Elizabethans inherited a tradition of play-acting from the Middle Ages, and they reinforced this by reading and translating the Roman playwrights. At the beginning of the sixteenth century plays were performed by groups of actors. These were all-male companies (boys acted the female roles) who travelled from town to town, setting up their stages in open places (such as inn-yards) or, with the permission of the owner, in the hall of some noble house. The touring companies continued outside London into the seventeenth century; but in London, in 1576, a new building was erected for the performance of plays. This was the Theatre, the first purpose-built playhouse in England. Other playhouses followed, including the Globe, where most of Shakespeare's plays were performed, and English drama reached new heights.

There were people who disapproved, of course. The theatres, which brought large crowds together, could encourage the spread of disease – and dangerous ideas. During the summer, when the plague was at its worst, the playhouses were closed. A constant censorship was imposed, more or less severe at different times. The Puritans, a religious and political faction who wanted to impose strict rules of behaviour, tried to close down the theatres. However, partly because the royal family favoured drama, and partly because the buildings were outside the city limits, they did not succeed until 1642.

Theatre

From contemporary comments and sketches – most particularly a drawing by a Dutch visitor, Johannes de Witt – it is possible to form some idea of the typical Elizabethan playhouse for which most of Shakespeare's plays were written. Hexagonal (six-sided) in shape, it had three roofed galleries encircling an open courtyard. The plain, high stage projected into the yard, where it was surrounded by the audience of standing 'groundlings'. At the back were two doors for the actors' entrances and exits; and above these doors was a balcony – useful for a musicians' gallery or for the acting of scenes '*above*'. Over the stage was a thatched roof, supported on two pillars, forming a canopy – which seems to have been painted with the sun, moon, and stars for the 'heavens'.

Underneath was space (concealed by curtains) which could be used by characters ascending and descending through a trapdoor in the stage. Costumes and properties were kept backstage in the 'tiring house'. The actors used the most luxurious costumes they could find, often clothes given to them by rich patrons. Stage properties were important for showing where a scene was set, but the dramatist's own words were needed to explain the time of day, since all performances took place in the early afternoon.

A replica of Shakespeare's own theatre, the Globe, has been built in London, and stands in Southwark, almost exactly on the Bankside site of the original.

Shakespeare's Globe, Southwark, London, England. Photograph by Richard Kalina.

William Shakespeare, 1564–1616

Elizabeth I was Queen of England when Shakespeare was born in 1564. He was the son of a tradesman who made and sold gloves in the small town of Stratford-upon-Avon, and he was educated at the grammar school in that town. Shakespeare did not go to university when he left school, but worked, perhaps, in his father's business. When he was eighteen he married Anne Hathaway, who became the mother of his daughter, Susanna, in 1583, and of twins in 1585.

There is nothing exciting, or even unusual, in this story; and from 1585 until 1592 there are no documents that can tell us anything at all about Shakespeare. But we have learned that in 1592 he was known in London, and that he had become both an actor and a playwright.

We do not know when Shakespeare wrote his first play, and indeed we are not sure of the order in which he wrote his works. If you look on page 161 at the list of his writings and their approximate dates, you will see how he started by writing plays on subjects taken from the history of England. No doubt this was partly because he was always an intensely patriotic man—but he was also a very shrewd businessman. He could see that the theatre audiences enjoyed being shown their own history, and it was certain that he would make a profit from this kind of drama.

The plays in the next group are mainly comedies, with romantic love-stories of young people who fall in love with one another, and at the end of the play marry and live happily ever after.

At the end of the sixteenth century the happiness disappears, and Shakespeare's plays become melancholy, bitter, and tragic. This change may have been caused by some sadness in the writer's life (one of his twins died in 1596). Shakespeare, however, was not the only writer whose works at this time were very serious. The whole of England was facing a crisis. Queen Elizabeth I was growing old. She was greatly loved, and the people were sad to think she must soon die; they were also afraid, for the queen had never married, and so there was no child to succeed her.

When James I came to the throne in 1603, Shakespeare continued to write serious drama—the great tragedies and the plays based on Roman history (such as *Julius Caesar*) for which he is most famous. Finally, before he retired from the theatre, he wrote another set of comedies. These all have the same theme: they tell of happiness which is lost, and then found again.

Shakespeare returned from London to Stratford, his home town. He was rich and successful, and he owned one of the biggest houses in the town. He died in 1616. Although several of his plays were published separately, most of them were not printed until 1623, in a collection known as 'the First Folio'.

Shakespeare also wrote two long poems, and a collection of sonnets. The sonnets describe two love-affairs, but we do not know who the lovers were. Although there are many public documents concerned with his career as a writer and a businessman, Shakespeare has hidden his personal life from us. A nineteenth-century poet, Matthew Arnold, addressed Shakespeare in a poem, and wrote 'We ask and ask—Thou smilest, and art still'.

There is not even a trustworthy portrait of the world's greatest dramatist.

Approximate Dates of Composition of Shakespeare's Works

Period	Comedies	History plays	Tragedies	Poems
I before 1594	Comedy of Errors Taming of the Shrew Two Gentlemen of Verona Love's Labour's Lost	Henry VI, part 1 Henry VI, part 2 Henry VI, part 3 Richard III	Titus Andronicus	Venus and Adonis Rape of Lucrece
II 1594–1599	Midsummer Night's Dream Merchant of Venice Merry Wives of Windsor Much Ado About Nothing As You Like It	Richard II King John Henry IV, part 1 Henry IV, part 2 Henry V	Romeo and Juliet	Sonnets
III 1599–1608	Twelfth Night Measure for Measure All's Well That Ends Well Pericles		Julius Caesar Hamlet Othello Timon of Athens King Lear Macbeth Antony and Cleopatra Coriolanus Troilus and Cressida	
IV 1608–1613	Cymbeline The Winter's Tale The Tempest	Henry VIII		

Exploring *Othello* in the *Classroom*

Love, lies and double-dealing can all be found in *Othello*, but at its very heart is the 'green-eyed monster': jealousy. Young people studying the play will have no difficulty relating to these universal themes and ideas as they explore the ill-fated marriage between Othello and Desdemona.

This section suggests a range of approaches in the classroom, to help bring the text to life and engender both enjoyment and understanding of the play.

Ways into the Play

Students may feel an antipathy towards the study of Shakespeare. The imaginative and enthusiastic teacher, with the help of this edition of the play, will soon break this down!

What's in a name?

Before they embark on the play, give students a list of its main characters (see page xiii). For each name, ask students to decide on such aspects as the character's gender, age, nationality and occupation. This will help the students to become familiar with the names as well as prompting some thoughts about the characters. They can then compare their ideas with the descriptions of the characters at the start of the play. Where the information is not given (e.g. age), ask the students to look for evidence and clues in the text.

Pictures

Every picture tells a story, so ask your students to look at the picture on the front cover of this book and guess who the people are and what is happening. Once they are more familiar with the play, ask your students to hazard a guess as to the moment in the play that is depicted.

Navigating the Play

Your students may need some help and practice in finding their way around a Shakespeare play. After explaining the division into acts, scenes and lines, challenge them to look up some references as quickly as possible. Refer them to some of the famous lines and those that might lead on to further discussion of the plot. Below are some suggestions.

Act 1, Scene 3, lines 48–9	*Valiant Othello we must straight employ you*
	Against the general enemy Ottoman.
Act 3, Scene 3, lines 167–9	*O beware, my lord, of jealousy:*
	It is the green-eyed monster which doth mock
	The meat it feeds on.
Act 4, Scene 2, line 69	*Alas, what ignorant sin have I committed?*

Improvisation

Working on one of the following improvisations may help students to access some of the ideas behind the drama.

a) Ask students to create a scene between a parent and an older teenager. The teenager has done something of which the parent strongly disapproves (e.g. had a tattoo, dyed his/her hair blue, bought a motorbike). Ask students to improvise the scene where the parent finds out.

b) Dishing the dirt: two acquaintances (A and B) are talking about a third person (C). Acquaintance A has a high opinion of C, and B tries to break down this high opinion, without appearing to be nasty. What tactics does B try? Is B successful? How does A feel by the end of the conversation?

c) Put students in pairs. Give each pair a theme to discuss (e.g. last night's TV, or today's lunch) and give the students in each pair separate and secret instructions: one student should be friendly, open and conciliatory; the other should be distrustful, defensive and antagonistic. At the end of their conversation, discuss how it felt to perform each role. This activity should foreshadow the scenes showing Othello's distrust of Desdemona.

Setting the Scene

The scene of the crime

Before they have read or heard an outline of the play, engage students with a small mystery. Inform them that a young woman has been murdered, and ask them to piece together some of the clues and construct a hypothesis for the crime. Give the students, working in groups, a number of clues or pieces of evidence derived from the play, e.g. some confetti, a handkerchief, a sword, a pillow, an extract from a letter between two characters (e.g. Roderigo and Iago), a newspaper headline (e.g. 'Othello is a war hero'). In addition, give students some pertinent quotations from the play to aid their discussions. Ask each group to report back their ideas. You may choose to read the synopsis and/or commentary so that they can see how close they came to the actual story.

The Moor

Othello is frequently described as a 'Moor', which may mean he is from North Africa or possibly from sub-Saharan Africa. He is black – an African prince – and is an outsider in the urbane, sophisticated world of Venice.

Ask students to look for evidence in the first Act of how Othello is regarded as an outsider. Create a 'role on the wall' poster, with an outline of the character. Ask students to put their evidence on sticky notes and attach them to the poster.

Discuss the evidence for racism in their findings – how characters' words and actions discriminate against Othello because of his race and colour. For example, why is Othello often referred to as a Moor, rather than by his name? What impression do we gain of Othello before we see him? Should a modern performance of the play be changed to make it less racist?

Venice and Cyprus

There are two main settings for the play.
- Venice: a thriving centre of international trade and culture
- Cyprus: a Mediterranean island under threat of invasion.

Both settings would have seemed very exotic to audiences in Shakespeare's time, when foreign travel was experienced only by a few. Even today, these are lively and attractive locations. Show students some pictures that give a flavour of Venice and Cyprus today – or allow them time to do their own research. Ask them to design two different sets: one for a scene in Venice, and the other for a Cypriot scene. Their designs should aim to illustrate the contrast between the two worlds of the play.

Keeping Track of the Action

It is important to give students opportunities to 'digest' and reflect upon their reading, so that they may take ownership of the play.

Reading journal

As your students to read through the play; help them to trace and understand the plot by asking them to keep a journal in which they record what happens, as well as their reactions and thoughts about the action and the characters. Focus their responses by asking specific questions. Alternatively, ask the students to write diaries from one or more of the characters' viewpoints, perhaps giving different perspectives on the scenes.

The two-faced god

Janus was the Roman god of gates and doors. He was usually depicted with two faces and it is significant that Iago chooses this god to swear by. Janus looked both backwards and forwards. He was particularly worshipped on occasions involving beginnings and endings – for example, the start of a new year, marriage, and birth.

At the end of each Act, ask students to give Janus's report on what has happened and – using this knowledge – to predict what is going to happen. Encourage them to comment on what has happened and evaluate it. Their reports might be written or oral.

Emotional thermometers and graphs

Encourage students to chart the emotional temperature of the drama through thermometers or graphs. For the thermometers, create a 'thermometer template' – for example, a picture of a thermometer with a 20-point scale. The template can have thermometers for 'love', 'hatred' , 'jealousy', and so on. At key points in the drama, ask students to assess the level of hatred, for example, and colour in the thermometer at the appropriate level. Similarly, students can chart the emotional levels within scenes, through using a line or bar chart.

Film and image

Using a film of *Othello*, such as those listed in the Further Reading and Resources section, is a good and illuminating way to make the play accessible to students. DVD versions are particularly helpful, as clear still shots can be captured and analysed to show relationships and interpretations. Similarly, students can look at paintings and images inspired by the play – for example, those in the Shakespeare Illustrated, the Royal Shakespeare Company or other websites (details given in the Further Reading and Resources section) – as well as the illustrations and photographs of productions in this book.

Exploring different interpretations and treatments can give real insight into the work. Students working at GCSE level may be able to develop this into a piece of coursework that examines a director's interpretation of the play. Some students may like to create their own piece of artwork in response to the play.

Characters

Students of all ages need to come to an understanding of the characters: their motivations, their relationships and their development.

The villain

Iago is one of Shakespeare's nastiest villains. The audience is aware of his malicious intent, but he manages to deceive those around him with ease. Once he is apprehended, Iago – who has more lines in the play than Othello – refuses to say any more.

Ask students to imagine that Iago has agreed to be interviewed by a journalist from a tabloid newspaper. What questions will he be asked and how will he respond? Ask students to write up the interview in an appropriately sensational style.

Obituary

Othello follows the typical pattern of Shakespeare's tragic heroes: he is highborn and has good qualities; but his character also has a flaw. Bad luck and misjudgement lead to his downfall. His tragedy affects those around him, and he pays the ultimate price – death.

Ask students to write an obituary for Othello that reflects all of the elements of the tragic hero.

Character chatroom

If you have a school computer network, ask your technician to set up a 'message board' to discuss the characters and their actions. Discussing the characters in this way gives all students the opportunity to contribute, and prevents a few people from dominating the chat, as can happen in traditional classroom discussions.

Set up some thought-provoking 'threads' to which students can respond. For example:

- *Desdemona was sneaky in not telling her father she was getting married*
- *Othello should have been a better judge of the men under his command*
- *Othello was too quick to believe the worst of his wife.*

Make sure you moderate the message board to ensure that the contributions are appropriate and that everyone is involved. If you do not have such ICT facilities, set up a classroom message board, where the 'threads' are on large pieces of paper dotted around the classroom, to which students can add their thoughts using pen or pencil.

Themes

Jealousy

This play is possibly the greatest work of literature to focus on jealousy. Ask students to do one or more of the following:

- write a definition of the word 'jealousy'
- create a product called *Jealousy* (e.g. a magazine, a perfume, a game) and produce a poster advertising it
- devise a mime that shows jealousy
- create a poem or rap, based on the play, entitled *Jealousy.*

Theme grids

Encourage students to search for evidence of themes and key ideas by creating theme grids. Choose one idea (e.g. love, honesty, jealousy) per grid. Tell students to create a grid or table with the names of the characters appearing down the left-hand side and repeating the names along the bottom. Where the names 'meet' in the grid (this will be twice) students must give a relevant quotation and explanation for how the given theme affects these two characters. This can be used to help them prepare for an essay on a particular theme.

Programme

Ask students to design a programme cover for a production of *Othello* that reflects some of the main themes, ideas and motifs in the play: for example, love, marriage, deceit, pride, jealousy, a handkerchief. Remind them that the programme will also need to give essential information about the play and the production.

Shakespeare's Language

Double talk

With his command over words, Iago takes delight in manipulating the other characters in the play. His words are full of double meanings, and he often intends the very opposite of what he actually says. Iago slips into prose when his words are more informal or down-to-earth – a devise that is often used by Shakespeare. Ask students to study the following scenes and speeches that illustrate Iago's cleverness with words:

● Act 1, Scene 3, line 298 to the end of the scene. Note the use of prose to speak 'candidly' to the baser character Roderigo, the use of repetition, the many imperatives, how Iago reverts to verse at the end of his soliloquy, etc.
● Act 3, Scene 3. Note the uses of insinuation, suggestion, questions, irony, etc.

Heroic words

In the first part of the play, Othello speaks the language of a hero. He adopts the formality and refinement in his language commensurate with his noble status. He fits in easily with the civilized society of Venice. Guide students through an examination of his speeches in Act 1, Scene 3, lines 76–94 and 127–169. He has eloped with the daughter of a nobleman, yet he defends his actions as proper and justified. Students should look at how he achieves this. They can also compare these words with his less measured and calm words later in the play, when he raves jealously (Act 5, Scene 2, from line 257). Alternatively, they can compare Othello's simple sophistication with Iago's speech patterns (for example, in Act 2, Scene 3).

Soliloquy

Shakespeare uses soliloquies to reveal the true feelings and thoughts of his characters. Characters do not lie in a soliloquy. Iago's soliloquies are of particular significance in this play, for in them he reveals his true thoughts and plans only to the audience.

Ask students to look at one or more of Iago's soliloquies. Whereabouts do they tend to appear, and why? Encourage the students to consider:
- the effect of the soliloquy on the audience
- the relationship Iago builds with the audience through his comments and questions
- how Shakespeare builds the character of the villain
- how the audience can appreciate the 'depth' of Iago.

Finally, challenge students to write another soliloquy for Iago in the final scene, summing up his actions and reactions to what has happened.

Exploring with Drama

Book the hall or push back the desks, because the best way to study a great play is through drama. Students of all ages will benefit from a dramatic encounter with *Othello*. They will enjoy the opportunity to act out a scene or two, or to explore the situations through improvisation: for example, by putting a character in the 'hot seat' for questioning by others.

Tableaux

Ask your students to create a tableau, or freeze frame, which contains all the main characters from the play. The positions of the characters should say something about their relationships and positions within the play. Bring the tableau to life briefly by having each character say something in character. They might also make a prediction about what they think will be their future.

If you have access to a digital camera, you can photograph and print out the tableaux so that students can add 'thought bubbles' giving the characters' comments as well as evaluations of their drama work.

Reduced theatre

Test students' understanding of the plot by asking groups to create a reduced version of the whole play. They will first need to decide on the key events and the essential characters, and they should try to include some quotations in their version. It should be no longer than two minutes' long.

The trial

Ask students to create the trial of Iago. Students can be given different responsibilities: for example, lawyers, reporters, witnesses, jury, judge. Encourage them to examine the play for evidence.

A performance

Students may enjoy the opportunity to act out a significant scene from the play. Let them choose a director who will interpret and lead the performance. This speaking and listening work can be followed up with an evaluation of the scene and of Shakespeare's intentions, and their own interpretation and performance.

Writing about *Othello*

If your students have to write about the play for coursework or for examinations, you may wish to give them this general guidance:

- Read the question or task carefully, highlight the key words and answer all parts of the question.
- Planning is essential. Plan what will be in each paragraph. You can change your plan if necessary.
- Avoid retelling the story.
- *Othello* is a play, so be ready to consider the impact or effect on the audience.
- Use the Point, Evidence, Explanation (PEE) structure to explain points.
- Adding Evaluation (PEEE!) will gain you higher marks.
- Keep quotations short and relevant.
- Avoid referring to a film version of the play, unless this is part of your task.

Further Reading and Resources

General

Fantasia, Louis, *Instant Shakespeare: A Pratical Guide for Actors, Directors and Teachers* (A & C Black, 2002)

Greer, Germaine, *Shakespeare: A Very Short Introduction* (Oxford, 2002)

Hall, Peter, *Shakespeare's Advice to the Players* (Oberon Books, 2003)

Holden, Anthony, *Shakespeare: His Life and Work* (Abacus, 2002)

McConnell, Louise, *Exit, Pursued by a Bear: Shakespeare's Characters, Plays, Poems, History and Stagecraft* (Bloomsbury, 2003)

McLeish, Kenneth and Unwin, Stephen, A *Pocket Guide to Shakespeare's Plays* (Faber and Faber, 1998)

Muirden, James, *Shakespeare in a Nutshell: A Rhyming Guide to All the Plays* (Constable, 2004)

Wood, Michael, *In Search of Shakespeare* (BBC, 2003)

Children's/students' books

Carpenter, Humphrey, *More Shakespeare Without the Boring Bits* (Viking, 1997)

Ganeri, Anita, *What They Don't Tell You about Shakespeare* (Hodder, 1996)

Lamb, Charles and Mary, *Tales from Shakespeare* (Puffin, 1987)

McCaughrean, Geraldine, Stories from Shakespeare (Orion, 1997)

Websites

The Complete Works of Shakespeare
http://the-tech.mit.edu/Shakespeare/

Elizabethan pronunciation
Including information on insults.
www.renfaire.com/Language/index.html

Encyclopaedia Britannica – Shakespeare and the Globe: Then and Now
Information about the Globe and the theatre in Shakespeare's times.
http://search.eb.com/shakespeare/index2.html

Folger Shakespeare Library
Teaching and learning ideas.
www.folger.edu/eduLesPlanArch.cfm?cid=#50

Royal Shakespeare Company
www.rsc.org.uk/othello/about/home.html

The Shakespeare Birthplace Trust
Information on his works, life and times.
www.shakespeare.org.uk/homepage

Shakespeare's Globe
Information on the Globe Theatre, London.
www.shakespeares-globe.org/

Shakespeare High
A Shakespeare classroom on the Internet.
www.shakespearehigh.com/

Shakespeare Illustrated
An excellent source of paintings and pictures based on Shakespeare's plays.
www.emory.edu/ENGLISH/classes/Shakespeare_Illustrated/Shakespeare.html

Spark Notes: Othello
An online study guide.
www.sparknotes.com/shakespeare/othello/

Mr William Shakespeare and the Internet
A comprehensive guide to Shakespeare resources on the Internet.
http://shakespeare.palomar.edu/

Film, video, DVD and audio

Othello
Directed by Orson Wells (1952)

Othello
Directed by Trevor Nunn (1990)
Starring Ian McKellen, Willard White, Imogen Stubbs

The Animated Tales of Shakespeare
A boxed set of 12 thirty-minute plays (1992)